Popular Culture

KT-218-601

Carla Freccero

POPULAR CULTURE

AN INTRODUCTION

New York University Press

New York and London

NEW YORK UNIVERSITY PRESS
New York and London

Copyright © 1999 by New York University
All rights reserved

Library of Congress Cataloging-in-Publication Data
Freccero, Carla, 1956–
Popular culture : an introduction / Carla Freccero.
p. cm.
Includes bibliographical references and index.
ISBN 0-8147-2669-0 (cloth : acid-free paper)
ISBN 0-8147-2670-4 (paper : acid-free paper)
1. United States—Civilization—1945– 2. Popular culture—United
States—History—20th century. 3. Mass media—Social
aspects—United States—History—20th century.   I. Title.
E169.12 .F717 1999
306'.0973—dc21   99-6112
                                 CIP

New York University Press books are printed on acid-free paper,
and their binding materials are chosen for strength and durability.

Manufactured in the United States of America

10 9 8 7 6 5 4 3 2 1

To Generation X

and all my students

CONTENTS

Contents

ACKNOWLEDGMENTS

I could say right off the bat that it is impossible for me to thank here all the people who contributed, in one way or another, to the shape and completion of this book, but there are particular people I want to name for the crucial ways their persons, their thinking, their labor, and their love made the work possible. First, I thank my students at Dartmouth College and at the University of California, Santa Cruz, who took my Cultural Studies and Popular Culture course. Their skepticism, their vast knowledges of the domain of popular culture, and the energy they devoted to studying the popular inspired me and contributed vitally to my analyses.

I thank Nancy Vickers, who, at Dartmouth College in the years that we were colleagues together, taught me how much fun and how much work analyzing popular culture could be, and who first encouraged me to write about Madonna. Cirri Nottage and Melinda Weinstein acted as research assistants when I was writing about Madonna. Dana Blumrosen, who, as a student at UCSC, first took the course, then, as my research assistant, helped me organize the reading materials for another version of the course, also taught me a lot about popular culture, as did my teaching assistants, Tera Martin, Sergio de la Mora, Ana Rodriguez, and Michelle Habell. Robert Miotke helped me think through many of the cultural meanings in the films and videos I study and also acted as my research assistant in compiling materials on the *Alien* trilogy.

I thank Eric Zinner at New York University Press for his valuable suggestions and for the readers to whom he showed the book and who provided me with helpful critique and commentary. Also at New York University Press, Despina Papazoglou Gimbel and Daisy Hernández offered gracious and prompt assistance and suggestions. Grants from the Committee on Research of the Academic Senate of the University of California, Santa Cruz, enabled me to acquire the necessary research assistance to continue and complete the project. The Document Publishing and Editing Center at UCSC also provided considerable editorial assistance with the manuscript. Gracious and intelligent assistance—at the eleventh hour—was provided by Catherine Newman.

The book could not have been started or completed without the admirable research skills, patient faith, enthusiastic energy, and brilliance of two graduate research assistants in particular: Robin Baldridge and Liddy Detar. I owe them an enormous debt of gratitude and a serious share of the credit for this book's existence.

I wish to thank the artist Jamie Hewlett for granting permission to use the image of Tank Girl from The Odyssey series on the cover of the paperback edition of this book. In this picture, Tank Girl—a riot grrrrl version of Madonna for the post-apocalypse—sits sprawled on the couch amidst the detritus of late-twentieth-century popular culture with Booga, her kangaroo lover from the Australian outback. This queer cross-species, interracial alliance of persecuted and marginalized outlaws epitomizes a certain youthful white female Imaginary of risk and empowerment as it is reflected back by television's mass-mediated storehouse of images. As such, it serves as an emblem for the matter of analysis in this book.

Friends and colleagues throughout the years have shared my enthusiasm for the critical analysis of popular culture, and I hope I have acknowledged the places where their ideas gave birth to or refined my own.

ONE

Popular Culture

An Introduction

This book evolved from a course I first taught for the comparative literature program at Dartmouth College in the summer of 1992 and subsequently taught twice more in the literature department at the University of California, Santa Cruz; a representative syllabus is included in the appendix. These two contexts differed vastly, as one might expect. Dartmouth College is an elite, conservative, small, rural liberal arts college, whereas UCSC is a larger public research university in the University of California system known for its progressive, if not radical, ethos. Dartmouth might be seen to be on the front lines of the war against **political correctness**, while UCSC might be seen to be PC's main stronghold (words in boldface are defined in the glossary). Both institutions value excellent undergraduate teaching and hold their faculty to high standards of performance in the area of pedagogy, yet each institution requires that a very different sort of pedagogy be developed.

When I taught the course at Dartmouth, I kept in mind a horizon of conservative response to the materials and ideas I presented and was careful to make my points concerning U.S. ideology through close readings of texts, videos, and films, in order to demonstrate the ways these materials "spoke" their meanings, rather than give the impression that I was a liberal preacher imposing leftist political significance or judgment onto a text. For Dartmouth students, popular culture was a domain of degraded culture: it was not the culture they were there to learn, even if it was their culture. They thus provided me with the ideal opportunity to argue the case for the importance of treating popular culture and mass media as objects worthy of critical study.[1]

At UCSC, students were too ready to denounce the ideology of U.S. mass media productions, too ready to condemn their representations of **race**, gender (see **sex/gender**), and **sexuality**. These students also claimed the popular as their domain, often educating me on trends and cultural formations about which I had very little first-hand knowledge (grunge, raves, and Dead culture, in particular). What they did not have—and were self-conscious about—was the high cultural capital that would enable them to see the dialectic between the popular and the highbrow. They were, much more so than Dartmouth students, GenXers, deeply knowledgeable about the vocabulary (visual, aural, and linguistic) of mass media, what it "says" when it appears as a reference, in a film for example, but despairing of its ability to represent or produce anything more significant than the flotsam and jetsam of culture that it appeared to be. So these students gave me the opportunity to argue for the potential progressive productivity of mass media representations, and, on the other hand, to show them how **hegemony** works, not by shutting down all opposition, but by recognizing and incorporating it. The challenge at UCSC was thus to demonstrate the contradictoriness of popular culture—and liberalism itself—and tease out some of the ways a "conservative" message can speak against itself. At the same time, it became important, as at Dartmouth, to argue that popular cultural representations were as potentially complex and worthy of interpretation as the "great" canonical texts of European literature that were always being used to demonstrate the poverty of popular culture and of youth culture in general.

Why study popular culture, and why teach popular culture to college students? I believe there are many reasons to do so, but a simple answer to the question might be that the culture as a whole, or what is sometimes called "public culture" in the United States, already "studies" popular culture, that is, enlists it to explicate, argue, demonstrate, condemn, or praise this or that event or social phenomenon. Witness the debates around gay sexuality that have emerged following the April 1997 "coming out" episode of ABC's sitcom *Ellen* or, more recently, references to the film *Wag the Dog* (1997) to explain Bill Clinton's strategic bombing of purported terrorist targets in the Middle East as a means of deflecting attention from the investigation of his affair with Monica Lewinsky. Popular culture itself, especially in its commodity form, even generates political and cultural debates, such as the media discussions of race and racism occasioned by Warren Beatty's filmic satire about race and party politics in America, *Bulworth* (1998). In other words, popular culture is already, in our culture, seen to be of consequence: it is thought to influence (young) people—to both determine and reflect the values and beliefs of a generation—and it is also perceived to be a political arena, a place where certain ideas are advocated and others are condemned. Therefore, an obvious reason for studying popular culture is to be politically literate, to understand what issues are at stake when political leaders and others condemn or praise its representations.

A second reason, perhaps more pedagogical in motive, stems from the particular literacies of today's college students. When Allan Bloom, in *The Closing of the American Mind*, excoriated higher education in the country for the ignorance of college students, he held them to the literacy standards of his own day, as did E. D. Hirsch, in his less vitriolic and more well-meaning *Cultural Literacy*. What such a focus revealed were the noncompetencies of college-educated students: they did not share a canonical set of literary references from which to quote; they were not schooled in techniques of memorization and thus could not quote Shakespearean soliloquies (many of which themselves were once deemed "popular" culture); and they did not have the standard "social studies" or civics lessons of just a generation or so ago. Many of these developments can be explained historically: pedagogical methods have shifted away from memorization, for example. More important, perhaps, the historical shift away from a widely accepted notion that America is a homogeneous and singular culture (whether the image is of a melting pot or the mass production of uniform citizens from ethnic differences) has meant that students do not in fact share a single literary canon or a patriotic knowledge of government. Rather, they may be aware of several canons and the cultures of several nations. This is the phenomenon we have come to refer to as multiculturalism, and it is to a large extent taken for granted—although not always accepted—by students in high schools and colleges today. It produces a different and far less uniform set of competencies and literacies.[2]

In addition to a different set of cultural competencies, students share a literacy different from that of many, if not most, of their teachers, one that could be called technological.[3] In this electronic age, most students know more than their teachers about computers, video, CD-ROM, the Internet, the World Wide Web, television, and the entire domain of telecommunications, and often have greater access to such technologies at their educational institutions. Thus they develop literacies that are unfamiliar to those schooled primarily in print or oral (verbal) culture; most students I know "read" postmodern visual texts more competently and more quickly than most teachers I know. They are more at ease with fast-moving fragments of knowledge and information than those of us who were taught to compose coherent bodies and fields of knowledge from what we learned.

Thus an approach to learning through popular culture enables students to recognize and draw on their already existing literacies and the cultures they know in order to analyze and think critically, skills that may be expanded and applied to other, less familiar domains. What students have learned outside the classroom are the techniques of acquiring information from media, the technological processes that inform their production, and how to go about obtaining access to the technologies themselves—how to "consume" them. This is what advanced capitalist culture successfully teaches. What the cultural studies approach to popular culture in the classroom can provide, then, is an approach to technological cultures that seeks to understand the social meanings of the representations produced by these cultures: a way, in other words, to analyze these products. The result will be not only an "informed consumer" but someone who may be able to intervene to produce meanings in the language of the medium itself and intervene politically when those representations are used to support particular agendas.

As long as popular culture remains a degraded cultural form in the minds of liberal educators and students themselves, it will be available for use without analysis, much the way religion and morality are invoked in U.S. public culture as givens without meanings that are subject to contestation. Liberal arts education will will itself into anachronism—as it is already being accused of doing—by focusing exclusively on forms of cultural production that are not widely shared in public culture. The domain of popular representation will pass as fact, unavailable for argument, debate, and analysis, or it will become an arena of technocratic competence where the focus will be on how to manipulate or manage it, but not analyze and interpret it.

My approach, which combines my extensive and traditional training in literary study with the newer field of cultural studies and its popular objects (**subcultures**, mass media, popular music, popular fictional genres, including science fiction and mystery novels), treats the objects of study as "texts" to be "read," even when those objects are not necessarily written texts. I start from the premise that all representations tell a story, more than one in fact, and that representations can be read or interpreted the way one would interpret a written narrative. Representations are made up of **signs**, and together these signs combine to tell a story; the first—that texts consist of signs—I call the semiotic dimension of texts, and the second—that signs, in combination, tell a story—the allegorical. **Semiotics**, the study of signs, allows one to treat the elements of a representation—any representation—as a set of signs that signify something to someone, that point beyond themselves to a range of other meanings, which are in turn partially determined—and limited—by their social context. In the case of popular culture, that context is U.S. public culture (the culture of the late-twentieth-century United States), which includes aspects of everyday life, politics, economics, history, and the social, as well as the more limited notion of culture, the artistic and anthropological dimensions of a society. If we accept the premise that representations are also allegorical, that is, that they tell multiple stories and that those stories are not only the explicit story represented by the plot (of a given film, for example), then it is possible to argue that the stories that such representations tell are stories about the culture from which they emerge. They are, I argue, political, psychic, and social.

Written texts, however, are privative; they deprive the reader of the sights, sounds, smells, gestures—in short, all the paralinguistic details that round out the meaning of anything we seek to understand. Their underdetermination means that certain conventional figures or **tropes** will have to do the work that, in live communication, is provided by the context. This is called the rhetorical dimension of literary language. Whereas other media may benefit from the paralinguistic, contextual details that allow one to determine meaning in a fuller way, they, like literature, each follow a set of conventional guidelines for signifying that make up for the specific constraints of the medium, whether these constraints are technological (as in film, where three-dimensionality must still be represented by two-dimensional means) or sensory (music, for example, when it does not have words to enrich its signifying codes). Thus it is also important, when "reading" media, to understand the rhetorical conventions or devices that govern their signifying practices. We are all familiar with the convention in horror movies, for example, of using a certain kind of music to signal to the audience the presence of danger or the imminence of an attack.

Perhaps because written text is so obviously deprived, or because, simply, my training is literary, I find that the rhetorical devices and the techniques for their interpretation developed in the field of literary study are the most complete available for analyzing any medium that relies on a specific set of restricted means of communication. These techniques of close reading and interpretation that are attentive to social and historical context enable many kinds of analysis, such as those that attempt to chart the workings of the psyche (**psychoanalysis**), or those that assess the political investments of representation (ideology critique or historicism).

The literary is not the only domain from which such an analysis can emerge: cultural studies is a field that combines a wide range of disciplines in an interdisciplinary manner. These include, among others, anthropology, sociology, communication studies, film studies, and political theory. Cultural studies may also take as its object a wider range of phenomena than I choose to examine here, and thus may require other techniques than the primarily literary ones I use. For example, population surveys, audience studies, news and television analyses all require specialized skills that the study of cultural representations does not necessarily include.[4] My focus here, then, is on the kinds of representations amenable to those skills I have developed, skills that fall within the general category of a liberal arts education: reading, writing, critical thinking, and qualitative analysis.

This book may be said to take as one of its organizing principles a certain phenomenon within popular culture that David Glover and Cora Kaplan have named "the fate of the sixties-within-the-eighties." In "Guns in the House of Culture" they write,

> Today the fate of the sixties-within-the-eighties is a notoriously important issue in the struggle for cultural and political meaning, an instance of the way the conflicting forces in every conjuncture attempt to write uncontestable histories for themselves. The hegemony of the New Right has involved a sustained critical attempt to monopolize the complex terrain of the popular, and in particular to drastically overhaul the social significance of the sixties. (222)

I understand the "sixties" here to refer to a wide range of political and social struggles in the United States and elsewhere. Some of the significant social movements for subsequent decades and for the popular cultural productions I look at in this book are the civil rights movement, Black Power, Black nationalism, and the **identity politics** that took their inspiration from them (including Chicano nationalism, the American Indian Movement, second-wave feminist movements, women of color movements, lesbian and gay rights movements). National liberation struggles and the decolonization movements of the sixties in the Third World also influenced and shaped many of these domestic social struggles. The baby boom generation and the student upheavals of the sixties, which can be said to have given rise to the term "counterculture" in the United States, figure importantly in the popular cultural imagination of the eighties and nineties, as do the Vietnam War and the assassinations of the Kennedys, Martin Luther King, Jr., and Malcolm X. Needless to say, this list is not exhaustive, but a quick survey of MTV videos from the eighties would demonstrate that these moments (in the form of newsreel footage and photographic images from the sixties and seventies) in sometimes confused and always fragmentary form, contribute to the cultural imagination of current youth and public culture today.[5] The "sixties-in-the-eighties," and, I would add, in the nineties, thus inform both the issues guiding this study and the content of the materials included in the book.

As Glover and Kaplan note, the eighties ushered in a national conservativism and a right-wing backlash against what was viewed as the excessive liberalism of the previous decades; the "backlash" also includes, importantly, a polemic against the sixties. George Will, writing for *Newsweek* in 1991, illustrates the extent to which the political and social significance of the sixties—and popular culture that is seen as "nostalgic" for that decade—becomes a political target for neoconservative polemic:

> [Jim] Morrison was not [Arthur] Schlesinger set to music, but both were symptoms of a Sixties disorder. Schlesinger's words "expression" and "release" were part of the mantra of the decade that made Morrison a shooting star, and soon a cinder. The cult of self-validating expression contributed to the debasement of education, which came to be considered a process of letting something out of students rather than of putting something into them. The craving for "release" from reason and other intolerable restraints, led to the confusion of narcissism with freedom.[6]

Here, as elsewhere, popular culture becomes the currency of political polemic and debate. Meanwhile, popular cultural forms themselves contradictorily register both the adoption of and the backlash against values perceived as belonging to the sixties; for example, they may adopt "multiculturalism" as a value, even as they express resentment against the class aspirations of ethnic and racial groups that are not "white," or they may understand the claims of feminism even as they revel in the epithet "bitch." This is especially true of the mass media forms I analyze here: Hollywood films such as *The Silence of the Lambs* (1991), *Basic Instinct* (1992), *The Bodyguard* (1992), *Waiting to Exhale* (1995), *Dead Man Walking* (1995), and the *Alien* trilogy (1979, 1986, 1992). One lesson to learn from mass media representations is, then, that they are politically contradictory. What I seek to encourage in readers of these texts is the ability to **articulate** the ideological work they perform and to identify gaps of logic and contradictions where the cultural critic might intervene to tease out progressive elements from within the **dominant culture**, and to understand how hegemony recognizes and incorporates counterhegemonic energies.

Ultimately I am interested in practicing cultural politics, strategically developing what Andrew Ross calls the **protopolitical** in popular culture, particularly in those media that have been derogatorily designated as "mass culture" or the "culture industry" by left- and right-wing intellectuals alike. It is my general feeling that the Left cannot retreat into anachronistic puritanism with regard to what it calls the new opiate of (young) people—"mass" culture—or else it cedes a strategic terrain of cultural politics all too clearly recognized as such by the New Right. These texts may suggest strategies for the empowerment of the subordinated, marginal, and decentered in advanced capitalist culture, strategies that are not anachronistic but born of the medium of advanced capital and the gaps that are produced within it. I am interested in the way such strategies, and such technology, may be used to produce significant counterhegemonic forces within a culture whose ruling classes seem to have perfected the art of containment.[7] The degree to which this is possible in any given text varies widely, and I do not underestimate the extent to which such a project is limited by both the institutionalization of cultural studies in U.S. universities and the increasing marginalization of humanistic studies in universities in our culture. Popular culture is a currency, however, that circulates between the academy and public culture, and as such it can at least constitute a common terrain of contestation.

This book also studies popular culture that more closely resembles the definition of the popular as that which belongs to the people. Texts such as Jewelle Gomez's *Gilda Stories*, Octavia Butler's *Xenogenesis* trilogy, Sandra Cisneros's *Woman Hollering Creek*, and William Gibson's *Neuromancer*, and films and videos such as Marlon Riggs's *Tongues Untied* or Jennie Livingston's *Paris Is Burning* can be said to constitute, to a certain degree, oppositional cultural productions that also rework the social insights of the sixties toward more politically progressive ends, in an effort to fashion radical social visions for the present and the future. Many of the cultural critics that I rely on to theorize these texts, such as bell hooks, can also be said to forge oppositional cultural energies.[8] These texts thus demonstrate that the popular is also explicitly engaged in counterhegemonic cultural practices in the name of participatory democracy, and that it can challenge neoconservative public culture's representations of the people.

I have therefore organized the chapters of my book according to the social formations and issues—feminism and sexuality, multiculturalism, and **technoculture**—that, in eighties and nineties terms, interpret the social legacies of the sixties within the framework of cultural studies, the academic field that has focused most prominently on these issues from a leftist point of view. In teaching the course on Cultural Studies and Popular Culture, I chose to organize these topics in such a way as not to separate the interstructured and co-articulated components of what I take to be some of the most vital categories of contestation in public culture: race, gender, class, sexuality, and, in a different but equally contestatory manner, technology. Each chapter takes as its specific focus one or another of these, but endeavors not to exclude or elide the others from its analysis and, further, selects cultural representations that explicitly interweave them. While I have not devoted a chapter to the topic of feminism, the entire study is fundamentally informed by the political, social, and critical insights and practices of this political and theoretical movement, as it is also critically shaped by the legacy of Marxist politics and theory.

Each chapter deals with a set of issues relevant to the study of popular culture and performs readings of selected popular cultural texts. Chapter 2 discusses the field of cultural studies, provides some background, and raises some common concerns related to the question of representation: what does it mean to talk about "good" and "bad" representations? What is at stake in analysis versus judgment of such representations? I then go on to introduce the category of cultural politics through a reading of serial killer narratives and what they might have to say about popular ideological fantasies in our culture.

Chapter 3 first raises questions about recent efforts on the part of the state to legislate the conduct of bodies and their representations in public culture; here I discuss the relationship between censorship and representations deemed obscene or indecent. Since the completion of this book, new questions concerning the relationship between the state, sexuality, and the promulgation of "obscenity" suggest themselves as a result of the publication (in the press and on the Internet) of the Starr report (graphically) detailing President Clinton and Monica Lewinsky's sexual encounters.

I then go on to discuss the phenomenon of subcultures, using Dick Hebdige's well-known book, *Subculture*, as a point of departure. I focus on a particularly prominent subcultural formation in the United States today that I pluralize under the heading "sexual subcultures," or what also might be called "**queer** culture." The readings in this section focus on sexual subcultures in Jewelle Gomez's *Gilda Stories* and the most famous recent representer of sexuality, Madonna. Toward the end of the chapter I argue for the interstructuredness of representations of gender, sexuality, and race.

Chapter 4 concerns itself centrally with the cultural and political movements most associated with the question of "race" today: identity politics and postcoloniality. I use Jennie Livingston's film *Paris Is Burning* and the cultural critic bell hooks's response to the film to explore the question of race as it is related to sexuality and gender. This chapter is largely historical and theoretical; it concludes with a reading of Octavia Butler's *Xenogenesis* trilogy as an example of a fiction that combines the domestic issues of race as it is understood in the United States with the thematics of **colonialism**.

Chapter 5 further explores identity politics, this time focusing on some theories of **hybridity** promoted by Chicana feminists and others, while also analyzing popular cultural representations of gender, race, and racialization: Sandra Cisneros's *Woman Hollering Creek* and Spike Lee's *Do the Right Thing*, rock, as well as rap, and pop. This chapter thus also deals with notions of resistant or oppositional culture as they are expressed in music; it presents a case study for the analysis of political and cultural ambiguity by analyzing the relationship between several popular films (*The Bodyguard, Waiting to Exhale,* and *Dead Man Walking*) and their soundtrack albums. These too have something to say about race, gender, and sexuality in our culture.

Finally, chapter 6 discusses another important dimension of our "**postmodern** condition": technoculture. This chapter introduces readers to understandings of postmodernism and explores the question of technoculture through feminist analyses of technology and through the science fiction genre of **cyberpunk**, here represented by one of its "founders," William Gibson. It asks questions about the constitution of virtual communities of the future, given the youthful **homosocial** fantasies that much of virtual reality seems to represent. It concludes with an extended reading of the ideological fantasies embodied in the first three *Alien* films, demonstrating what a cultural politics approach to representation might yield in the way of understanding cultural anxieties and fantasies about race, gender, reproduction, sexuality, and technology.[9]

Readers of *Popular Culture* will find my choice of works to examine and issues to analyze idiosyncratic; indeed, the domain of the popular is so vast that no one could hope to cover its range of cultural productions and the numerous political and social debates it mobilizes. My choices have been guided, in part, by debates arising in public culture during the years that I was teaching this course and writing the book, and I would hope that any study of current mass media and popular culture—particularly in the classroom context—would do the same, for these are the debates and the cultural productions that capture the energies of students. Nevertheless, I hope that the approaches employed, the issues discussed, and the readings presented will serve as a useful and effective springboard from which other kinds of courses on, and studies of, popular culture may emerge.

There is one reason for analyzing and teaching popular culture that I have not mentioned thus far—seeking, as I was, to persuade the reader of the seriousness and importance of such a study—and that is pleasure. Pleasure is frequently, if not always, the disavowed motivation for even the most serious and scholarly of studies, studies that denounce the assertive and playful pleasures of popular culture as frivolous.[10] Emma Goldman declared that she did not want to belong to a revolutionary movement where she could not dance, and her statement points to the ways pleasure—and its sources in fantasy—are powerful mobilizers of the political. Since popular culture has the audacity to make pleasure (or "enjoyment," as Slavoj Žižek calls it) its purpose, cultural studies and the study of popular culture can inspire students and intellectuals to affirm the pleasures of critical analysis, to confront not only the cultural politics of pleasures, but also the pleasures of cultural politics.[11]

TWO

Cultural Studies, Popular Culture, and Pedagogy

A. Overview and Background

In England, where cultural studies originated, its disciplinary center was sociology. Perhaps most influential to the later American development of the field was Stuart Hall, a Black sociologist who directed, for a time, the Center for Contemporary Cultural Studies in Birmingham.[1] In its inception, cultural studies grew out of the experience of educating working-class people with a commitment to the political applications of knowledge and criticism; it was also therefore committed to a kind of theorizing and critical practice that had social change as one of its goals. It took as its object of study the everyday culture and practices of people.

The definition of "culture" for cultural studies comes from the British Marxist critic Raymond Williams, who argued that culture is a whole way of life (ideas, attitudes, languages, practices, institutions, structures of power) and a whole range of cultural practices: artistic forms, texts, canons, architecture, mass-produced commodities, and so on. Culture means the actual grounded terrain of practices, representations, languages, and customs of any specific historical society. Culture, in other words, means not only "high culture," what we usually call art or literature, but also the everyday practices, representations, and cultural productions of people and of **postindustrial** societies.[2]

According to Grossberg, Nelson, and Treichler, the editors of the influential anthology *Cultural Studies*, the term "cultural studies" covers a range of theoretical and political positions that use a variety of methodologies, drawing on **ethnography**, anthropology, sociology, literature, feminism, Marxism, history, film criticism, psychoanalysis, and semiotics. Cultural studies is anthropological, but unlike anthropology, it begins with the study of postindustrial rather than preindustrial societies. It is like **humanism**, but unlike traditional humanism it rejects the distinction between so-called low culture and high culture and argues that all forms of culture need to be studied in relation to a given social formation (4). It is thus interdisciplinary in its approaches. Cultural studies "has grown out of efforts to understand what has shaped post World War II societies and cultures: industrialization, modernization, urbanization, mass communication, commodification, **imperialism**, a global economy" (5).

I am using the concept of "popular," with which cultural studies is largely concerned, to talk about the everyday terrain of people without being sure who the people are, that is, without deciding ahead of time and once and for all who is being referred to by the term "people." I am also using it in the sense of "mass" culture, the popular cultural forms produced through the medium of mass technology and communications, as well as those forms produced on a smaller, localized scale. I will continue in this work the traditional focus of cultural studies on the disempowered or marginalized within a dominant culture and the ways struggles for power are conducted through representations. These groups are sometimes called subcultures (originally a term used in Britain to refer to youth cultures): cultural formations within the dominant culture that can be distinguished by a stance, a style, an attitude, a position, and a fashion as defiant, resistant, or oppositional to what is viewed as the dominant culture.[3] But the focus here will also be on the ways mainstream culture reacts to, defines, and represents certain subcultures.

What distinguishes cultural studies, above all, from other fields is that it has a commitment to examining cultural practices from the point of view of their intrication with, and within, relations of power. That is where politics comes in: cultural studies is not a "politically neutral" discipline. It is also a bridge between theory and material culture, and a focus on the social difference that theory can make (*Cultural Studies*, 6). Analysis depends on intellectual work; but intellectual work is incomplete unless it enters back into the world of cultural and political power struggles. This book thus is not about the transcendence of art, its universality, its message to all humankind; it is about the relationship between cultural artifacts (movies, videos, science fiction books, comic strips, pornography, popular novels, popular science, performance art) and our social order; and it is also about various "subcultures" in the United States and their cultural productions. A cultural studies approach seeks to understand what culture has to do with the economic, political, and social forces that structure and order our lives depending on who we are and where we are located in the social order. Another way of referring to this positioning is "situatedness," or someone's "subject position," as empowered, disempowered, permitted, proscribed, visible, invisible, privileged, discriminated against, and so forth.[4]

As Michele Wallace (*Invisibility Blues*) and bell hooks (*Yearning*) argue, the representation of marginalized groups of people or subcultures in mass media has become a major arena of contestation in our culture. hooks points out that representatives of these groups of people have less access to the production of such images, and thus one way to have a voice is to challenge the dominant culture's representation of themselves. Both hooks and Wallace complain that much of this criticism takes the form of talking about "good" or "bad" images, which treats representation as a reflection of fact and suggests that there is one accurate way to represent a person from a minority group or a marginalized group. And to do this is to immediately buy in to the logic of stereotypes—that is, the logic of racism, sexism, or homophobia—by accepting the mass media's capacity to "represent" a group of people.

One of the challenges in dealing with media representation is not only to decide whether representations are good or bad, but to analyze them. What work are they doing? What motivates the representation? What does this representation say about the representers and the imagined viewers of such a representation? What elements are combined in a cultural representation? What contradictions get highlighted?

Asking some of these questions is a way into a cultural studies analysis of a mass media–produced visual text. How does it speak about the social context that produces it? Michele Wallace's remarks on close reading and context are useful here: "however 'close' that reading may be, it won't provide much information about how literature by black women alternately conspires with and rebels against our present cultural and political arrangements."[5] Thus she calls for "cultural reading" (656) as an act of resistance, whereby cultural productions are consistently tied by the reader to social, historical, and political contexts.

The question of the politics of any popular culture text—whether or not it challenges dominant ideas about the culture—is always difficult, and it often risks becoming a version of the good and bad representation issue; but we may still explore the possibilities and limits of such texts. In order to be truly popular, texts must appeal across a broad range of political and subject positions. For example, until recently, the mass culture industry did not seem to realize that Black culture was a marketable commodity and that there were enough middle-class African American consumers to constitute a serious consumer population.[6] Racism functioned in a very contradictory manner here: because market analysts thought white people would not be interested in Black films or Black music, there was very little of it in Hollywood or on MTV; because they thought all African Americans were poor, they also didn't think there was enough of a Black consumer market for Black films, Black ads, Black MTV. Now the industry knows it was mistaken. One could describe this as a positive or negative development, and in fact it is both. On the one hand, protests from Black constituents and the entry of African Americans into Hollywood as directors forced a change in the industry. On the other hand, Black culture has now become a commodity like any other, one that does not, by and large, profit African Americans. This commodification, by managing race relations, increases the possibilities for control as well.

Popular culture representations, in their most popular or mass form, often bear contradictions within them and send very mixed political messages, covert messages, or even unconscious messages, so that a variety of people can consent to them. Consider why some movies have failed to attract a large market, and you will see that it is often because the politics were too clear or the message too extreme. This is mostly true for representations that are oppositional, that is, representations that take an unpopular stand against widely held beliefs or political positions in the culture.[7] This also explains why it is still possible to make very racist or sexist movies: there is still enough of a constituency to support such representations in the culture, and the people targeted do not yet have enough visibility or voice to challenge the representations in question. What, then, are popular culture's possibilities for challenging the social order? What limits these possibilities, and why?

As Stuart Hall argues, cultural studies "has to analyze certain things about the constitutive and political nature of representation itself, about its complexities, about the effects of language, about textuality as a site of life and death."[8] By "the constitutive nature of representation" he means the way representations (visual, aural, verbal, etc.) actually construct their object, so that rather than talking about good or bad images of something that exists "out there" in its true or authentic state, we need to talk about how an image constructs what it is representing. We have to pretend, in a way, that we do not know what that object is (a lesbian, for example, in a film such as *Basic Instinct*), and we must ask, how does this representation construct lesbian identity? The political nature of representation may be a clearer concept to grasp: how, for example, do representations affect the lives of the people and situations they represent? How do they influence decision making about their subject matter? (Take the *Murphy Brown* show, for example; or *The Silence of the Lambs*—how does this representation of a pseudo-**transsexual** man influence the politics of queer struggle for rights and recognition?)

This project is also about changing our position as "mere" consumers of mass culture and making us into critics, meaning that we approach our culture critically and we analyze it, not only in order to denounce it, but in order to understand the ways it works on us, the ways we are implicated in it. It is about understanding how our culture represents us and how we are represented in it. Thus, this kind of analysis also always involves locating oneself as analyst: what is your subject position; how are you situated in relation to it and by it (how does it situate a person as consumer, reader, viewer, participant, addressee); how is any given representation about you, speaking to you or for you, that is, how does it construct you as the consumer of that representation? This is an easier critical consciousness for some than for others. For example, as hooks says, there has always been a tradition of critical consciousness in African American communities in the United States because of U.S. policies explicitly disenfranchising such communities. If you know that the dominant culture is not "for" you or "about" you, it is easier for you to view it with a critical eye. So too, says hooks, it becomes difficult to be critical of (to critique) a representation when it is produced by "one of your own" (she gives the example of Spike Lee), because the representation claims to speak for you and about you, in your name and in your interests. But whether the work is easy or hard, critiquing is one of the most important things to do.[9]

We also, all of us, change subject positions. There are times when we will be explicitly "othered" by a representation, just as there are times when a representation is for us and "others" someone else. The point is to be aware of this rather than unreflectively responding to it. Here is where the concept of **"interpellation"** or "hailing," developed by the French Marxist philosopher Louis Althusser, is very helpful. It refers to how a social formation constructs us as subjects who respond and consent to it in certain ways. It is a description of how ideology functions, not by persuading us with rational argument to believe that something is true, but by manufacturing our consent to certain ideas by representing them as self-evident reality.[10]

John Fiske's essay "Cultural Studies and the Culture of Everyday Life" introduces some of the key notions in cultural studies: the idea of culture as the culture of everyday life; the idea of the *habitus* or social space that locates us in terms of cultural and economic capital, education, class, and history (*Cultural Studies*, 155). He makes the important point that material, everyday lived culture is a contradictory mixture of creativity and constraint: "The social order constrains and oppresses the people, but at the same time offers them resources to fight against those constraints" (157). Elizabeth Young's essay "*The Silence of the Lambs* and the Flaying of Feminist Theory" illustrates what Fiske is talking about: how the film offers creative critiques and possibilities for the questioning of gender even as it constrains and oppresses us within its models of gender.[11] "The constraints," Fiske writes, "are material, economic ones which determine, in an oppressive, disempowering way, the limits of the social experience of the poor. Oppression is always economic. Yet the everyday culture of the oppressed takes the signs of that which oppresses them and uses them for its own purposes" (157). Here we might want to think about how classic Hollywood representations of the ultimate in femininity, Marilyn Monroe, for example, become cult and camp icons for gay male subcultures, who often feature drag performances of these famous Hollywood stars.

Fiske also discusses the body as the site of social control (161–62). To say that the body is a site of social control is to make the point, first and foremost, that the body is not some kind of natural biological entity, but an artifact, a socially constructed, socially situated body acted on by a host of interrelated **power-knowledges**. This concept was popularized by the French historian and philosopher Michel Foucault, who analyzed how social formations organize technologies of power and knowledge (psychiatry, police, prisons, hospitals, medicine, science, universities, governments) that are mapped onto bodies and construct us as subjects.[12] The body is no longer conceived of as a bundle of raw instincts and impulses that law, order, and government are supposed to discipline but that always threatens to break loose; rather, the technologies of discipline and surveillance construct us as beings who think we are "repressed" and in need of sexual "liberation," in order to create an economy of management and social control. Serial killer movies, which I will be discussing later, illustrate this managed, surveilled body very well, by linking together representations of the police, psychiatry, knowledge, power, and techniques of surveillance.[13]

Thus, for example, we come to believe that sex is an arena of transgression and liberation as opposed to order and reason; we come to believe that we must discipline ourselves to be productive citizens, and yet that abandoning ourselves to sexual impulse is a form of liberation from that discipline and control.[14] As long as we believe this, we have no reason to question the ways the institutions of our society channel us into narrow corners of liberation and in actuality succeed in "managing" us even more. (Rousseau argued that women could never be citizens because they could not discipline, control, and sublimate their sexuality.)

This is a very pessimistic view. Another dimension of the social I would like to explore is how people, in turn, resist their management by technologies of power-knowledge. One way might be through a cultural studies approach. As Stuart Hall says, there is something at stake in cultural studies ("Cultural Studies," 278)—and perhaps what is at stake is human liberation from the various ways we are managed, controlled, surveilled, that is, the ways we are interpellated by **ideology**. A kind of liberation can be at least partially achieved through a critical analysis of our culture and the ways different domains of life interconnect, through the production and practice of critical knowledge. This means questioning our own assumptions every bit as much as we question the assumptions of others and of the cultural objects we examine and analyze. Hall argues that one of the goals of cultural studies is the formation of the organic intellectual (a term that comes from Gramsci) and the development of intellectual and theoretical work as a political practice (281).[15]

After Hall presented his paper, a conference attendee asked him whether he was proposing an elite model of learning, where people are divided into a class of intellectuals who do the analyzing, on the one hand, and the rest of us, on the other (290). But cultural studies attempts to work against this model of an elite class of educated people that holds knowledge and rules the world with the extra knowledge it has. The idea, then, would be to develop a kind of knowledge and critical practice that all could share. This is why, as hooks and Wallace point out, popular culture is so useful.[16] Everyone already does share it as an arena of cultural contestation and discussion. Recent political debates in the United States and debates about censorship and public funding for so-called obscene art have centered around artifacts of popular culture: debates on important social issues have arisen as a result of Madonna, the rap group 2 Live Crew, Spike Lee, Sistah Souljah, *Murphy Brown*, Ice-T, gangsta rap. These popular culture texts have been at the center of nationwide critical debates about sexuality, motherhood, racism, homophobia, freedom of speech, pornography, cultural differences, and multiculturalism.

Toward the end of his essay on the theoretical legacies of cultural studies, Hall expresses a fear that if cultural studies becomes too institutionalized—particularly as it has done in the United States—it might begin to ignore questions of power, history, and politics.[17] hooks also echoes this concern: "Many academics involved with cultural studies do not see their work as emerging from an oppositional, progressive, cultural politic that seeks to link theory and practice, that has as its most central agenda sharing knowledge and information in ways that transform how we think about our social reality" (*Yearning*, 6). On the other hand, she also endorses cultural studies analyses of popular culture:

> Much postmodern engagement with culture emerges from the yearning to do intellectual work that connects with habits of being, forms of artistic expression, and aesthetics that inform the daily life of writers and scholars as well as a mass population. On the terrain of culture, one can participate in critical dialogue with the uneducated poor, the black underclass who are thinking about aesthetics. One can talk about what we are seeing, thinking, or listening to; a space is there for critical exchange. It's exciting to think, write, talk about, and create art that reflects passionate engagement with popular culture, because this may very well be "the" central future location of resistance struggle, a meeting place where new and radical happenings can occur. (31)

My position, like theirs, is both hopeful and skeptical: when we talk about mass culture or electronic culture, we are talking about a culture enmeshed in systems of mass production and consumption, multinational corporations and systems of international capital. This knowledge tempers any excessive optimism about the progressive potentials of popular cultural representations, reminding us that all these cultural productions are involved to some extent in technologies of social control.

Political positioning is clearly crucial to cultural studies; in the case of the present work, it will be clear that I occupy a particular political position rather than posing as neutral or bias-free in my analysis of the cultural texts in question. Thus, some of the critiques may raise political objections from readers. There is no question that cultural studies as a whole, with a history of Marxist and otherwise oppositional critique, has a leftist political agenda at its core, and it would not make sense to pretend that that is not the case. But to be oppositional and progressive or to have as one's goal social change does not mean giving up rigorous analysis and lucid critique, as is implied in the term "political correctness." In a context where the hegemonic culture is right-leaning, being oppositional raises a challenge to be even more critical, even more lucid, even more self-questioning than those in power, who do not have similar stakes in social change. It is not enough to assert that something is so—it must be argued in ways that persuade or convince.

In teaching cultural studies, hooks asks,

> Am I educating the colonizer/oppressor class so that they can better exert control? . . . [my friend] says that we can only respond to this circumstance by assuming a radical standpoint and radicalizing students so that they learn to think critically, so that they do not perpetuate domination, so that they do not support colonialism and imperialism, but do understand the meaning of resistance. (132)

This is an ambitious project that no theoretical enterprise could hope to accomplish without an activist practice to test it, and this is perhaps the greatest classroom challenge to an intellectual endeavor that sees progressive political change and intervention as one of its goals: the U.S. college classroom does not easily accommodate activism. Given the constraints, "critical thinking" may nevertheless prove invaluable, and achievable; in other words, universities today are still in a position to promote this aspect of participatory democracy.

Critical analysis can be assisted by practices of close reading; close reading here means noticing everything in a text, but it also means not adding "speculation," "psychology," or our own opinions, beliefs, and ideology to that text. It means, in other words, making an argument about meaning based on evidence that can be found in the representation itself. Critical self-awareness in this regard means knowing the difference between reading what is there and adding something to a text from one's own intellectual and experiential baggage. This is not to say that one's own opinions and speculations have no value, but that it is important to distinguish between those and what is in the text itself. This is a very difficult distinction to make in practice, not the least because public discussions in our culture almost never do. For example, if Sistah Souljah says, "whites beware," Bill Clinton translates that as "Sistah Souljah counsels blacks to hate whites"; this is an example of what I call ideological reading (to be distinguished from a reading that is attentive to ideology), reading something into a statement that is not there.[18] The exercise of critical analysis is, rather, about exploring the possible meanings of what *is* there, delaying, in other words, the tendency to use a representation to promote one's own ideology, beliefs, and prejudices.[19]

B. Serial Killers and the Question of Representation

I want to begin with a popular genre of representation in mainstream culture, the serial killer story, to illustrate some of what might be included in a cultural studies approach to popular culture, specifically in relation to film. I refer to three films in particular, *Dressed to Kill* (Brian de Palma, 1980), *The Silence of the Lambs* (Jonathan Demme, 1991), and *Basic Instinct* (Paul Verhoeven, 1992), which, because of the fame of their actors or directors, became **crossover** films that appealed to and were viewed by a wider audience than the usual "horror" genre fans. These three films bring together a nexus of concerns that relate to mainstream culture's anxieties around violence in the culture, feminism, and newly recognized sexual subcultures and sexualities.

A cultural studies discussion of films such as *Basic Instinct* focuses on aspects of the film that would not necessarily be covered by a strict film studies analysis, and does not look at this film as one would for a film studies class. Questions of formal genre (such as how *Basic Instinct* is a camp "anthology" of the **film noir** genre, citing Hitchcock, among others) and its relation to the classic police detective narrative, while relevant, do not constitute the main focus of my discussion. Instead, I would propose looking at how *Basic Instinct* puts gender roles into play; for example, one could situate this film in the context of the women's movements of the last twenty years and explore the way it seems to react to those movements by talking about how women have

| 23 |

become rich, dangerous, and educated (both Catherine and Elizabeth, the film's heroines, have master's degrees from Berkeley) at the expense of "ordinary" (working-class) white guys.

Basic Instinct is an interesting film to consider in the context of cultural politics because it was the object of intense debate about questions of gender and sexuality. The film offers us a representation of bisexuality or lesbianism, and it has served as an occasion for debates about the representation of gays and lesbians in the media, debates that often take the form of interrogating whether a particular representation is "good" or "bad" (politically, socially) for the people it represents. But as I mentioned, such debates do not ultimately analyze the representation in question. In the case of *Basic Instinct*, what seems to get represented most around the question of bisexuality or lesbianism is its exclusionary nature, the way it refuses domination or control or access by straight men. This movie tells us a lot, in a tongue-in-cheek way, about straight male anxiety and paranoia—in other words, we laugh at the male hysteria in this film even as we share it. Is this because, as some read the movie's ending, there is really nothing to worry about from the in-control, bisexual woman, because she is really just like any other woman and will fall in love with you (the straight white male) and submit to you, if only you prove yourself strong enough and persistent enough? This is the conclusion one arrives at if the ending is read as a narrative of domestication, that is, that the protagonist decides not to kill Nick because she loves him. Or does the movie really empower the independent woman who resists such control, and argue that indeed men are fascinated by the risky link between sex and death? If we follow this interpretation, then the "basic instinct" in this movie seems to be both the sexual instinct and the instinct to kill or to risk death, so that we could also see this movie as a kind of allegory about sex in the age of AIDS, imagining that the risk of death adds excitement (by adding lethal danger) to the question of sex.

Some of the popular debates about this film's "feminism" involved questions about the motives of representation: for example, is the portrayal of a rape tantamount to condoning rape? A representation is not automatically a recommendation. For example, some people argued that the portrayal of Nick forcibly having sex with Beth (Elizabeth) made *Basic Instinct* an antifeminist film. This statement does not, however, provide us with enough contextual information to come to such a conclusion. One would have to argue that the film suggests that force was justified, that Nick was right, in other words, to do what he did. I think one needs to make that case in order to argue that the film lends consent to the notion of rape.

Many people argued the antifeminism or homophobia of *Basic Instinct* on the basis of its representation of lesbians as pathologically angry murderers and drug users. But when one analyzes systems of sexual difference as they are represented in the culture, it is important not to isolate one side of the term in one's analysis. In other words, how is Nick represented in the film? Is he the good guy? Are white men good in the film? What does it mean that he is represented the way he is? It is also important to locate the subjectivity of the film, to figure out whose point of view is privileged and how this shapes our reactions, responses, and interpretations. Asking questions like these is a way into a cultural studies analysis of a mass media–produced visual text. How does the text speak about the social context that produces it? Does it challenge dominant ideas in the culture? What I am interested in here are the possibilities and limits of such texts.

In serial killer films we also witness a certain construction of a sexual category—the homosexual—and the traces of its longtime association with sexual **perversion**. The serial killer is a study in psychopathic perversion: he is usually a man with a sexual dysfunction, and in the eighties and nineties this has come to be associated predominantly in public culture with some form of homosexuality. The films mentioned—*Dressed to Kill, The Silence of the Lambs*, and *Basic Instinct*—demonstrate a newfound and self-conscious awareness of this identity category, an awareness based in recent efforts by gays and lesbians to win recognition and civil rights. It is just such an awareness that makes these films interesting as symptoms of mainstream culture's reaction to post-Stonewall political struggles for visibility, for they uneasily negotiate between "healthy" and "pathological" constructions of gay identity.

Dressed to Kill introduces a "new" category of socially recognized pervert, related in the culture's mind to homosexuality: the transsexual man. In the film, the multiple personality of the killer is split between the one

| 25 |

who wants to be a woman and the one who wants to stay a man. The one who wants to be a woman becomes a killer each time the man becomes sexually aroused as a man (the framework is **heterosexist** throughout, that is, it equates heterosexual desire with "being a man"). The problem, says the movie, is when you cannot make up your mind which you are or want to be. At the end of the movie, the biomedical technology of sex change operations is described luridly to the teenage male heroic protagonist of the film by the gutsy call girl who also solves the mystery. The audience is supposed to regard this procedure as monstrous.

In *The Silence of the Lambs*, the message has become more subtle: the problem is not authentic transsexualism or gender dysphoria, but the mistake of thinking that you want to be a woman when you are—and really wish to remain—a man. This film, in turn, confuses the categories of the gay person and the transsexual and suggests to us (through the name of the dog, Precious, and through the history of the killer and his male lover) that being gay, if you are a man, is the same as wanting to be a woman. Although the film hides behind the "mistake" that confuses the killer Jamie Gum ("Buffalo Bill"), it nevertheless invites our **voyeuristic** fascination with sexual subcultures: Jamie's dressing up, his hiding his penis between his legs and his mirror-image **drag queen** poses, his makeup, and of course, most obviously, his nipple ring all conjure up images of gay subcultural "lifestyles." These images collapse icons and elements of various sexual subcultures into a nexus that links homosexuality, transsexualism, female impersonation, perversion, and killing. *Basic Instinct* also displays confusion regarding the sexual subculture it purports to reference, although one might argue that this movie does not deal with being gay as a subcultural phenomenon, but rather isolates the lesbians/bisexuals, so that one does not have the impression of a culture that supports them at all.

Amy Taubin makes an argument about how and why serial killer stories are so popular in the United States:

> With just 5% of the world's population, the US is believed to have about 75% of the world's serial killers.
>
> Disturbing as these figures are, the fact is that the number of people who will die at the hands of serial killers doesn't even bear comparison with, for example, the number of women who will die because they

don't have access to breast screening, or even know it exists. But institutionalized violence—the destruction of millions of lives through poverty and neglect, the abuse practiced against women and children, the slaughter of 100,000 Iraqis—has no easy representation. The stage of the serial killer acts as a substitute and a shield for a situation so incomprehensible and threatening it must be disavowed.[20]

The popular fascination with random, illogical, and individual psychologically motivated violence is a reassuring fiction for people because it does not focus our attention on institutionalized social violence—violence that is motivated by reasons we see all too clearly (poverty, discrimination, etc.). At the same time, we acknowledge, on some subconscious level, that violence saturates our social order; but we displace it from its economic and political roots onto the figure of the psycho serial killer. This is one of the meanings of "seriality": the repeated nature of the violence points beyond the isolated incidents of violence toward the notion that violence, in our culture, is pervasive and repeated.

In order to further develop this issue of the "privatization" or "individualization" of violence that Taubin claims motivates the fascination with serial killers, we may find it useful to sketch the historical development of the ideology of liberal individualism. To call individualism an ideology is to argue that one must account—historically, as well as in other ways—for a phenomenon that, when we see it enacted in representation, presents itself to us as self-evident reality.

The liberal **bourgeois** political tradition, which was developed in Europe in the eighteenth and nineteenth centuries and corresponds on an intimate level to the economic system known as **capitalism**, constructs individuals as the primary entity in society. This represents a kind of cellular view of the body politic, where the whole is made up of autonomous, almost self-sufficient and independent entities who, acting together, form the whole body and motivate its actions. In fact, some feminist historians of evolutionary biology, such as Evelyn Fox Keller, have launched a critique against just this picture of the functioning of the human body, pointing out that it is not possible to take a cellular view of living organisms because most of them, particularly humans, never function in a way that isolates one cell. Cells are part of a system, and so to talk about them in isolation (the way, for example, sociobiologists talk about "the selfish gene") is an ideological notion derived from the bourgeois political tradition, one that conceives of humans as isolated individual beings who together, but also independently, make up what we call society.[21]

People are never found apart from a social order, and there is no such thing as an isolated individual. Yet our political tradition, our laws, our political philosophies assume precisely this model of humanity. Karl Marx argued that economics is always a political economy, that people exist in societies that have overall economic systems organizing the whole of the social order. He argued that we need to organize our economies as systematic and collective means for producing, distributing, and consuming the resources of groups of people, with a view to providing for the group, since it is only by virtue of our grouping together—our social existence, in other words—that we have economies. We do not live in isolation and we can collectively plan for the provision of the group. Yet classical economics (what motivates capitalism's economic philosophy) acts as though people are individual agents in individual economic transactions, even though all of us are wholly interdependent. And a corporation (you can even hear it in the word—from *corpus* or body) is simply viewed as a macrocosm of individuals.[22]

Thus, even though economies are completely interdependent and interrelated, we think of economic transactions as isolated events, actions committed by autonomous individuals acting as free agents in their own interests, as though each of us only coincidentally lived next to each other, and our existence was in some fundamental way independent from the existence or survival of other humans. Today, of course, we critique this notion with arguments about our entire interrelatedness, not just to other human beings, but also to organic life as a whole system: animals, plants, and the earth.

I have been making this argument to show how individualism produces a specific way of conceptualizing human beings and their interrelations in society that is not necessarily the truth of our social existence. We are never not social. Yet the way we talk about individuals assumes that people can be thought of as autonomous, independent, isolated, and above all—and this seems to be one of the greatest ruses of individualism—free.

Serial killers typify this individualistic conception of violence, as being located in a body, a single individual, as having primarily psychic causes, having to do with a private history, and as posing a very individualized threat to each and every one of us. The solution to the problem of violence, then, also becomes individual and private.[23] In serial killer stories we learn that the source of violence and disorder in the individual stems from his family, a family that is similarly dysfunctional for reasons not construed as social or political. The sources of pathology are located in a family history, a family romance, separable somehow from the rest of what goes on in the social order.[24]

Another contemporary example of this phenomenon of the privatization of violence is the recent focus on "child abuse" as the cause and source of our psychosexual disorders in contemporary U.S. society. This is represented in the movie *The Silence of the Lambs*, when Dr. Lecter says that Buffalo Bill was not born, but made, through years of systematic childhood abuse. Child abuse theories often seem to argue that we become monsters because of something that happens within the private sphere of the family. The person responsible is a specific, localizable individual: one or both of our parents is directly responsible, in other words, for the monsters we turn out to be. This is a picture of society that implies that we begin our lives and grow up in isolated private cells called families, disconnected from the rest of the social order and, indeed, from the rest of the world. At a certain point in our lives we then emerge into the public, bringing with us the damage done to us in this thing called the family. I am exaggerating somewhat, but I do so to show how these theories have a particular and ideologically specific view of the world that does not necessarily correspond to something we might want to call truth, and that they are theories with interested ideologies, that is, they tell a story of the way things are and present that story as self-evident reality. All stories are constructed: they are all particular versions of "the way things are," and they limit the possibilities of other stories being told even as they permit certain conclusions to be drawn.

What interests do these ideologies of violence serve? What are the implications and the consequences if we think of violence as something that originates in the private sphere, as a result of the actions of isolated individuals upon other isolated individuals (especially if it happened when those individuals were children)? What are the implications for dealing with the question of what Taubin calls "institutionalized violence" in the social order? What do they say about what the problem is, and what the solution to the problem might be? In the case of serial killers, individuals who threaten other individuals, the solution seems relatively simple: kill the serial killer and your problem goes away.

According to Taubin,

> Unlike urban action pictures, which imply that the threat to America is ghettoised, serial killer films are set in white neighborhoods—suburbia, the farm belt, the back woods. And in fact, almost all serial killers are white males who kill within their own racial group. Bred in the heartlands, he's the deformed version of the American dream of the individual. (16)

What does it mean to locate the "deformation" of the American dream not in corrupt government, in economic institutions that exploit us, or in systemic corruption, but in an individual?

If this is the general gist of serial killer narratives, then how does *The Silence of the Lambs* buttress this view of the world and the sources of violence in U.S. society, and how does it depart from the model outlined? Can this departure be at all described as progressive? Taubin wants to make the argument that *The Silence of the Lambs* is doing something special with this narrative by suggesting what we already know: that violence in our society is not a primarily individualized thing, that it is not only located in specific individuals with localizable and private sources, but in a whole legacy and history of American culture.

The Silence of the Lambs is, Taubin remarks, "packed with 300 years of relics—of white America. Every time Lecter sends Clarice on a treasure hunt—to a storage warehouse for example—she finds a flag or two tucked away with the rusty rifles, dressmakers' dummies and the odd severed head preserved in a jar. The flags look as though they've seen better days."

> Near the end of the film, in the aftermath of Clarice's battle with Buffalo Bill, the camera lingers for a moment in a corner of the killer's lair,

now lit with a shaft of light from a window broken in the struggle. First, there's a medium shot of a child's size American flag leaning against a dusty army helmet and then a close-up of a sea-blue paper mobile with a butterfly design—a bit of Chinatown interior decoration or a trophy from Viet Nam. Bill's inheritance and his legacy. Which is why the final image of Lecter after his murderous escape, sauntering down a crowded main street in Haiti [*sic*] resplendent in his creamy tourist suit, is more disturbing than anything that has come before. The serial killer, an American gift to the third world, a fragmentation bomb, ready to explode. (16)

Taubin's interpretation brings into view a possibly progressive, political reading of this film. This is what is meant by the term **disavowal** and how it functions: one knows that something is true, but one refuses that knowledge and constructs a cover story for that which one refuses to know. Thus one both knows and does not know "the truth." To foreground disavowal as a structure within representation allows us to identify and discuss this recognition of institutionalized violence in our culture and makes it possible to link stories of individualized pathology to the social.

THREE

Sexual Subcultures

A. The Body and the State

Before turning to the ways sexuality and sexual subcultures are represented in popular media (and I take as my starting point the peculiar representation of "gay" sexuality proffered by the recent serial killer films I mention in chapter 2), I would like to provide background on the recent political struggles for sexual rights in the United States in relation to efforts to censor popular expressions of sexuality. These struggles highlight the particularly fraught relation between the state and the body.

What follows, then, is a meditation on the question of the body and representations of the body and its relation to the state. The popular representations of sexuality and sexual subcultures I examine address the question of the body, the female body in particular, and its relation to issues of state control and male domination, issues of politics and the question of public versus private, the personal and the social. Most Americans are familiar with the fact that senator Jesse Helms has conducted a campaign to terminate public funding for so-called obscene art.[1] This has given new political impetus to sexual subcultures, as theirs is some of the work that has come under attack.

"There is more than one kind of freedom, . . . Freedom to and freedom from. In the days of anarchy, it was freedom to. Now you are being given freedom from. Don't underrate it."[2] Here Margaret Atwood depicts a future state, Gilead, where women are no longer the frequent victims of rape, forced sterilization, sexual abuse, and potential sexual degradation by exposure to pornography or other sexist representations of women's bodies. Women now live in a state where they have "freedom from." Sound ideal? The catch is that women can no longer own property, vote, or freely associate; if they are fertile they have no rights over their wombs: they cannot choose not to have children, nor can they choose to be gay or straight, or to marry and to whom. In short, women no longer have "freedom to," civil liberties or political rights. In Gilead they are protected by a strictly **patriarchal** and paternalist state that claims total ownership of their bodies. They have become, literally, state property.

Atwood's feminist dystopia explores the potential consequences of the appeal to state protection that is a current and familiar dilemma in the struggle for civil or political rights. You may recognize the dilemma in all rights movements, in all struggles with the state for recognition. The civil rights movement invoked the protection of federal law against the laws of individual states and the practices of the so-called private sector; feminist movements similarly sought protection at the federal level against family abuse and the private sector; the gay rights movement has sought to include itself under the umbrella of federal protection against discrimination. In all these struggles, people have appealed to the state for protection, the same state that has been responsible for their oppression or has, at least, colluded in it. The recent battles around the issue of federal funding for "obscene" or indecent representations are a case in point: the same people who appealed to the state to protect such art through funding now contend against the state's attempt to restrict (limit) the content of such art.

People grant the state the power simultaneously to legislate the conduct of bodies in public, the public body, or the body politic, and to protect the rights of private bodies. Thus people ask their state simultaneously to protect them and not to interfere with their liberty, establishing (ideally anyway) an uneasy equilibrium between the public aspect of bodies and the private. In other words, it's not as though current government intervention is a new phenomenon; there has always been a relation between the body and the state, a relation that involves greater and lesser degrees of intervention in the form of regulation and protection. In practice, of course, no state is as neutral as this picture makes it sound, and there are contradictions.

A history of the relation between the body and the state would first ask the question, whose interests does the state serve? There are bodies (children, animals, plants) and there are bodies. Our state serves the interests of bodies called citizens, which, at our state's inception, were defined as male adult property owners. Their incorporation as a state—or ruling class—was designed to safeguard their private property and regulate the lives of the rest of the people. The struggles I mentioned earlier form part of the history of people's battles with the state to force it to recognize their bodies as rights-bearing citizens. The importance of these struggles cannot be overestimated: they make the difference, for humans, between slavery and enfranchisement. As long as African American men and women remained only bodies in the eyes of the state, they had no rights. As long as the wives and daughters of citizens were bodies who belonged to their husbands or fathers, they had no rights. Animals do not have these rights, and children are still in between. Non–property owners have fewer rights than those who own property. Gay bodies are not enfranchised, while fetal bodies have emerged as a new category to contest the incompletely recognized rights of female bodies. Even when these struggles are partly successful, there are still enormous contradictions in the way the state recognizes the rights-bearing individuality of bodies: a body has rights only when it is understood to resemble or be identical to an adult male heterosexual and white property owner.

One way to recount the history of the relation between the body and the state is to look at the struggles of bodies to be recognized and protected, to explore the resulting contradictions, and to assess various strategies that attempt to change a state that is fundamentally hostile to those rights. This is the way I see it; for me, the state has a continuing interest in supporting the claims of white adult male (heterosexual) property owners over the claims of the rest of us.

An example of the dilemmas rights movements face when they confront the state is the feminist antipornography movement in the early to mid-eighties. It received a lot of publicity in the national press at the time, and more recently it has been invoked by right-wing legislators and other politicians as they pursue restrictive policies with regard to the representation of bodies and sexuality in the media and the arts.

Why did feminists focus on pornography as a site of women's oppression? My understanding of this is that it was in part a tactical decision. Women recognized that pornography was not the sole or most serious oppressor of women, but it was a highly visible representation of the way women are sexually degraded in the culture. Moreover, pornography occupies a vulnerable place in the law and in the culture. Most, if not all, states regulate sexually explicit representations, and there is a long history of debate about pornography and other sexually explicit representations in the United States. Thus legislation was already in place to facilitate an attack on the pornography industry, namely, obscenity laws, and public sentiment was mobilized against pornography, though for diverse and often contradictory reasons. The state itself maintained a contradictory position on pornography: on the one hand, elite adult men's right to consume pornography in private was protected, while the production, distribution, and consumption of pornography by the so-called masses were severely restricted and heavily regulated.

The most nationally visible political attempt to attack the pornography industry as agent of the sexual subordination of women was the antipornography ordinance coauthored by Andrea Dworkin and Catharine MacKinnon, acting as consultants to the Minneapolis city attorney's office in 1983. The MacKinnon/Dworkin pornography ordinance sought to make damage by pornography actionable in a civil procedure (by an individual woman claiming damage to herself or by an individual woman in the name of all women). One goal was therefore to render economically costly what was perceived as a form of sex discrimination. Another goal was to create a gap in the legal system where women could insert themselves—their voices, their agencies—and begin to structurally modify the patriarchal stronghold embodied in U.S. law. An admirable strategy by any feminist account. But was the tactical decision to apply pressure in the particular area of sexuality and its representations so clearly advisable?[3]

What were some of the accomplishments? The feminist antiporn movement heightened public consciousness of what had traditionally been a private matter, and in doing so exposed other "private" practices as matter for public politics: wife battering and violence against women generally, sexual abuse of women and children, and sexual violence. They put these issues on the national agenda, in other words. They **deconstructed** the tenets of constitutional "freedom of expression" by exposing the collaboration between a given social order and the forms of expression it is willing to protect, and they pointed out that representation and act are not always so clearly different. The public circulation of hard-core and violent pornographic materials as objects of study also enabled many to understand the concept of systemic sexual subordination through its explicit representations. In addition, many (middle-class) women who had never been exposed to what was viewed by the ruling class as an all-male preserve got to "see" it and speak out about it, often in "mixed" company, and this was empowering.

What are some of the problems? Much of the debate about pornography and sexual practices moves between the poles of civil libertarianism (the "liberal" position) and moral absolutism (the antiporn position of the New Right). Neither position specifically addresses the interests of women conceived as a political category. Civil libertarianism advocates the protection of the domain of the "private" from public intervention by the state, advocating therefore a minimum of state interference in personal liberties. But feminist sexual politics targets precisely the domain of the "personal" or "private" as one in which much of women's oppression takes place. "The personal is political" undoes a strictly libertarian view of the personal by identifying what was once an invisible site of oppression as the focus of a politics. Moral absolutism, on the other hand, seeks a single standard of morality for the polity, and while some feminists indeed do align themselves with such a position, it is historically opposed to the liberationist theories at the roots of most feminisms and sexual liberation movements, since that standard has been Judeo-Christian heterosexual monogamous patriarchy. Moral absolutism presents the paternalistic view of women: that women are weak, vulnerable persons requiring the protection of a benignly patriarchal state, of good men against bad men, in other words. Women who do not fit this model (prostitutes, for example) are "bad" and thus deserve the harm that may come to them at the hands of other men. To summarize, the civil libertarian position assumes that women are the same as adult white men, that they are wholly free to consent or to refuse consent; it does not recognize the unequal distribution of power between men and women. The moral absolutists assume that women are completely different, wholly dependent on men and requiring male protection.[4]

The state has an interest in regulating sexuality in general and the sexuality of women in particular because, as I said, it protects the interests—property rights—of a ruling class of men. As regards sex in general, the state legislates and enshrines morality. It suffices to look at statutes that criminalize certain kinds of sexual behavior (sodomy in particular) to see that this is true. For example, in the *Bowers v. Hardwick* Supreme Court case, Justice Berger declared that "condemnation of those practices [sodomy] is firmly rooted in Judeo-Christian moral and ethical standards."[5] Furthermore, the state regulates, controls, or one might say protects women's sexuality because women are still considered somewhere between "property" and persons. Insofar as they are still property, the state has an interest in protecting their bodies from violation (or theft, as the term "rape" once meant) by other men (men who are not their husbands or fathers) and an interest in controlling their reproductive functions as the potential property of husbands.

The dilemma for feminists is how to ensure sexual rights for women while simultaneously acquiring freedom from male sexual domination—how to achieve both "freedom to" and "freedom from." The antipornography movement focused closely on the issue of "freedom from." It seemed to be saying that women should be guaranteed protection from sexual abuse first, and their sexual freedom and **agency** could be dealt with later, once they were safe.

An important criticism of this position came from sex workers themselves, women whose livelihood depended to some extent on the pornography industry and other related sex work, women who felt victimized not by the exploitation of their sexuality per se, but by the hazards of their working conditions, hazards exacerbated by state restrictions and regulations. When the sex industry goes underground, these women lose the potential to organize more vocally for equitable wages, health care, and safer working conditions. At a time when more and more women are entering the wage labor force, when poverty is increasingly feminized, and when jobs are scarce, these women argued, sex work may be preferable to other forms of wage labor and should be a viable option for them. Many of them have suggested a different tactic: rather than focusing on representation, on pornography as a commodity, rather than struggling to limit or censor it, women should struggle to improve the working conditions of those women involved, to empower women within the industry and give them more control over the production of sexually explicit representations. This, they argue, will better serve the interests of women and challenge the sexism of pornographic representations. Their example, I think, can be applied to other movements that limit their mobilization to political rights alone.[6]

I have been assuming all along for the sake of argument that there is a connection between sexist pornography and women's oppression. One might ask whether representations reflect or determine attitudes. If representations influence attitudes, it is not in any clearly predictable way. Different people can see the same thing and react differently. I have chosen to assume that the issue of pornography was chosen for its tactical convenience and not because it is understood to have a direct effect on women's oppression. Even if it does, I am not convinced that its elimination will be decisive in liberating women from oppression. The lack of economic rights, health care, and reproductive rights is currently jeopardizing the lives of women and children immediately and directly (though perhaps some of these issues have not yet become middle-class women's issues).

In the nineties, the political situation also looks different from what it was in the late seventies and early eighties because anti-obscenity and antipornography mobilization at the state level has been directed specifically against sexually explicit representations in general, gay sex, sex education in general, and education about safe sex practices in particular. Thus the negative consequences of this particular struggle for state protection now seem to outweigh the positive effects. State protectionist policies regarding women's bodies have also shown themselves to be more about returning women to the status of property than recognizing their rights as persons. I think these recent developments demonstrate that though it may be difficult, it is crucial to struggle against the state on both fronts simultaneously, to demand "freedom to" as well as "freedom from." The struggles today in this country that seem best to exemplify this approach in the area of sexuality are the sexual radicals' and gay rights movements, where, by necessity, people are fiercely demanding both state intervention and private liberty in the form of sexual freedom. They are unable and unwilling to sacrifice one or the other for what would be at best a partial freedom and at worst, none at all. One cannot, however, limit this struggle to sexuality; we have to fight to try to make the state serve the interests of all of its people; in other words, we have to fight to change it.

Sex is a new social antagonism. There are moves afoot to fully and finally dissolve the liberal public/private split that middle-class feminism initially attacked; these moves, meanwhile, by producing swift reaction by the law, call attention to the investments of the state in what liberalism has designated as the domain of the private. But as Chandra Mohanty (among others) points out, female immigrants to Britain and the United States, as well as women of color in the United States, never benefited from such a distinction in the realm of sexuality.[7] Sex, along with the right to bodies and pleasures and desires, is being publicly reclaimed as it is being publicly contested. Now not only the private body but also the body politic is being sexualized, or rather, its sexualization is no longer so insidiously hidden and disguised and its monolithic unitary sex is being contested. To bring bodies and pleasures and desires into the body politic is to make them available for democracy, the goal of sexual (as of any other) rights. Perhaps, through the political movements that have adopted the erotic as their domain of struggle, a further resistive pleasure can be discovered and reclaimed: a leap of imagination that would undo the individualistic conception of the body as bounded and prohibited from the exchange of bodily fluids with others; the discovery of pleasure as sociality, bodies and pleasures connected and exchanged.

B. Queer Subcultures

Dick Hebdige describes subcultures as groups within the dominant or hegemonic culture that express a relation of resistance, opposition, or refusal to the larger culture or the hegemonic culture, that is, the culture that expresses the ruling order of any given social formation.[8] Subcultures might be oppositional, but usually they are not. They do not directly challenge the hegemony, but do so indirectly or obliquely, through style: "The objections are lodged, the contradictions displayed, at the profoundly superficial level of appearances: that is, at the level of signs":

> The struggle between different **discourses**, different definitions and meanings within ideology is therefore always, at the same time, a struggle within signification: a struggle for possession of the sign which extends to even the most mundane areas of everyday life . . . commodities are open to a double inflection: to illegitimate as well as legitimate uses. These humble objects (safety pins, for example) can be magically appropriated; stolen by subordinate groups and made to carry secret meanings: meanings which express, in code, a form of resistance to the order which guarantees continued subordination.
>
> Style in subculture then is pregnant with significance. Its transformations go against nature, interrupting the process of normalization. As such, they are gestures, movements toward a speech which offends the silent majority, which challenges the principle of unity and cohesion, which contradicts the myth of consensus. Our task becomes to discern the hidden messages inscribed in code on the glossy surfaces of style, to trace them out as maps of meaning which obscurely re-present the very contradictions they are designed to resolve or conceal. (17–18)

In this section we will look at various sexual subcultures, that is, subcultures that have consolidated around sexual practices, sexual orientations, and sexual styles. Most of these groups do not cluster only around sexuality, they also cluster around various other markings that marginalize them from the norm in some way; for example, Madonna's movie *Truth or Dare* (Alex Kreshishian, 1991) and Jennie Livingston's *Paris Is Burning* (1990) explore **house cultures** in New York City, the Black and Latino gay male subculture of balls and houses. Finally, there is what Donna Haraway (adapting Trinh Minh-ha's phrase) might call the imagined sexual subculture of some "inappropriate/d others," figured in Jewelle Gomez's novel *The Gilda Stories* as vampires.[9]

The problem with the term "subculture" is the "sub-" in front of "culture" that makes it sound inferior or below. I use it in the sense of "underneath" as a political category, much the way the notion of "underground" used to be used: a social group that is both subversive of some of the dominant culture's cherished rules and oppressed by them, struggling for a different way to live. Subculture is expressed through style: clothes, practices, costumes, body markings, ways of gathering in public spaces, hairstyles, hair colors. The oppressed and rebellious status of subcultures does not necessarily mean, however, that the politics (rarely explicitly expressed) of a subculture falls neatly into categories like left or right. Think of skinheads, for example, or fraternities, and even, possibly, the subculture of female impersonation and the subculture of lesbian **S/M**. All these subcultures are problematic for the politics of leftists and feminists, as well as for the politics of Republicans and Democrats.

Gay and lesbian subcultures have existed in their consolidated urban form at least since World War II in the United States. But my focus here is on the visible emergence, in print and cultural production as well as in embodiments, of gay and lesbian subcultures in their late eighties and nineties forms, what is sometimes referred to as queer culture. "Queer" is still a contested term among the gays and lesbians who originally used it as a term of self-designation; it seems to have been an attempt to take a distance from the orthodoxies of a politically correct gay and lesbian culture that had a seemingly coherent definitional strategy (men who love men, women who love women) and politics.[10] It emerged most forcefully around the new militancy centered on AIDS activism and groups such as ACT UP and Queer Nation, a militancy that refused the dominant culture's requirements that homosexuals somehow give up their **radical sex practices** or be damned. Queer culture thus formed also in resistance to the moral puritanism that sought a rationale for its condemnation of homosexuality in the emergence of AIDS, which, according to this moral puritanism, resulted from a lifestyle that included radical sex.[11]

On the other hand, there was resistance in lesbian circles to the trend of lesbian feminism to move in an antisex direction, toward a kind of anti–male supremacist utopian sexuality that did not involve relations of power inequality and violence. The lesbian magazine *On Our Backs*, as well as the lesbian S/M organization SAMOIS, arose in response to this resistance and reclaimed transgressive radical sex practices such as sadomasochism, fisting, dildo penetration, and **role play-**

ing. Recent attacks on the National Endowment for the Arts by anti-obscenity activists such as Jesse Helms also gave new life to sex radicals and queers, as the public political discourse in the United States began to force advocates of sex radicalism to become explicitly politicized around the issues of sexuality.[12]

Thus the term "queer," in some sense, came into being to describe the disparate "inappropriate/d others" whose sexual practices and proclivities could not be made to fit the identity categories of either gay or straight, although gay/lesbian sexual orientations constitute the paradigmatic center for this non-identity category. Queer culture celebrates hybridity, celebrates the borderland between this and that, and also introduces notions of multiple identities, noncategorizable identities, conflictual identities that are at odds with the way we are in the habit of classifying things. As Haraway says, "To be inappropriate/d is not to fit in the taxon, to be dislocated from the available maps specifying kinds of actors and kinds of narratives, not to be originally fixed by difference. To be inappropriate/d is to be neither modern nor postmodern, but to insist on the amodern" ("The Promises of Monsters," 299).

One way of thinking about this is to relate it to James Clifford's notion of traveling cultures and the moving between that he is interested in examining within anthropology, so that what gets undone or unstabilized is the notion of fixing, or taxonomy as a classificatory system, or the notion of stasis, a fixity of place rather than movement.[13] That is also why bell hooks refers to feminism as feminist movement, to counter the stasis of a noun that seems to name a fixed thing that is there in its place once and for all.[14] Thus Haraway uses the metaphor of the interference pattern, something that diffracts rather than reflects, something that interrupts, not in an on/off way but in a way that produces an elsewhere.[15] Of course, queer cultures also play on the generic meaning of queer as "strange" or "odd."

Another way to look at the difference between queer and gay/lesbian is to see that difference in terms of political goals, that is, in terms of a specific relation to the state. Gay/lesbian movement has come to be identified with identity politics and the struggle to acquire or achieve "civil" rights toward the goal of equal treatment in the eyes of the law. The goal of this kind of identity politics is to become individuals possessed of the same rights, freedoms, and privacies as are currently enjoyed by (white male straight) citizens of the United States. Recognized marriages, equal protection in the workforce, and the right to privacy around sexual practices are some of the demands of a rights-based gay and lesbian movement. Queer, on the other hand, takes an explicitly outlaw position, refusing to address the state and promote the goal of eventual inclusion in the polis.

Jewelle Gomez's *Gilda Stories* is a popular novel about vampires, whose primary protagonists are both female and lesbian (although there are male vampires in the novel too, and some of the vampires, both male and female, are heterosexual). The novel might be classified as science fantasy, that is, a story that takes place across impossible spans of time and involves "otherworldly" beings. By figuring her characters as vampires and as "alternatively" sexual, Gomez creates a literary parable for queer culture. Vampirism, which has a long filmic and literary history of being connected to homosexuality, receives a positively valorized sexual—and racial—reinterpretation in the novel.[16] Vampires are figures of gay and lesbian "being" through their mode of reproduction, which, by virtue of being tied to blood, is a form of kinship, but one that involves an erotic choice and is produced nonsexually. Vampires also "pass" for human.

The novel begins with an epigraph by Audre Lorde, the renowned feminist lesbian of color poet, critic, essayist, and activist: "At night sleep locks me into an echoless coffin / sometimes at noon I dream / there is nothing to fear."[17] Most obviously this image invokes the vampire as that figure who sleeps in a coffin during the day to avoid the rays of the sun (here represented in their most intense moment, noon). "I dream there is nothing to fear" is an interesting reversal in this poem and in this novel, for in the folklore it is we the mortals who are supposed to be afraid of the vampire; at the same time there is the idea that the vampire fears the day. Traditionally, fearing the day is a characteristic of evil things, the things that love the night and terrorize those of us who fear the night. Thus binary systems (sun/moon, night/day, vampire/human, white/black) are invoked and inverted, so that what is usually understood to be the negative term of the binary is positively valorized. Immediately the allegory suggests itself: to be a person of color is to be figured as a vampire, the dangerous creature associated with the black night who preys on white folks and takes their lives.

But in the poem we enter the subjectivity of the vampire instead. When Lorde says that at noon she dreams there is nothing to fear, and that the coffin she sleeps in is echoless, she demonstrates that from the point of view of the vampires in this novel, mortals are the dangerous ones: the hunters and the slave owners. The sun, then, in this novel and for the vampire, might be said to allegorically represent the way sun-reason is described by Haraway, as the quintessential visual single-centered masculinist dream of reason, rationality, speculation, and centeredness ("The Promises of Monsters," 300); the night and the moon, on the other hand, are feminine, cool, not rational, not dominating or overpowering. One might argue that a simple inversion of the terms of domination does not change anything. Indeed it does not, but the vampire confuses our ability to line things up on either side of the good/bad divide. The vampire culture in *The Gilda Stories* is multiracial, including white; it is male and female, gay/lesbian and straight. Vampires are good and bad; they have power that can be used either way, for life or for death. They hunt and are also hunted. They are both the same and different from mortals.

Haraway aptly characterizes the genre of SF as a space for the sort of thought experiment Gomez conducts in *The Gilda Stories*:

Science fiction is generally concerned with the interpenetration of boundaries between problematic selves and unexpected others and with the exploration of possible worlds in a context structured by transnational technoscience. The emerging social subjects called inappropriate(d) others inhabit such worlds. SF—science fiction, speculative futures, science fantasy, speculative fiction—is an especially apt sign under which to conduct an inquiry into the artifactual as a reproductive technology that might issue in something other than the sacred image of the same, something inappropriate, unfitting, and so, maybe, inappropriated. ("Promises," 300)

The Gilda Stories is thus an example of a popular cultural representation that is explicitly resistive or oppositional in intent. Many of the popular written genres, such as the western, the detective novel, and science fiction, have been extraordinarily amenable to reworking by representatives of marginalized and subordinated groups or subcultures. Gomez allegorizes multiple identity categories, both sexual and racial, in an attempt to refigure current American dilemmas of prejudice and imagine a sort of resolution or escape from these dilemmas.

C. Madonna's Popular Bodies

Madonna is perhaps the best-known popular cultural figure whose career has, in part, been forged in the representations of sexualities, both "straight" and "gay," and who has consistently celebrated sexual explicitness in her performances. The challenges she represents to a monolithic notion of the body and its pleasures deserve mention precisely because progressives have been reluctant to support her, in part because she seems the very icon of postmodern consumer capitalism. Her mass popularity, multimillionaire status, and CEO ambitions make progressives suspicious. But these are the very contradictions of the popular within technocultural capitalism. As Andrew Ross notes, "We cannot attribute any purity of political expression to popular culture, although we can locate its power to identify areas and desires that are relatively opposed, alongside those that are clearly complicit, to the official culture" (*No Respect*, 10).[18]

What does Madonna do with bodies and pleasures? Several of her videos enact what Cindy Patton (*Sex and Germs*) has described as sex-positive identity, desire, practice, and subjective agency with a view toward constructing a context for post-AIDS "sensible" sex practices. The "Justify My Love" video (Mondino, 1990) portrays the erotic daydreams of a woman in a hotel who, along with the (male) addressee of the video, enacts a series of erotic fantasies that is like a catalog of "safe" radical sex practices. The video begins with the long-fingernailed Black dancer who acts as the magical narrative thread for scene-switching throughout the video. Madonna is fantasizing in the hallway of a hotel. She kneels down in the hall and begins to masturbate. Her boyfriend appears, coming into focus, a technique that often signals dreams in Madonna videos and in MTV signifying systems generally. Madonna marks the beginning of the series of scenes with an

"OK," stressing (specifically female) agency and the importance of choice in creating these fantasies, fantasies that include heterosexual intercourse, heterosexual female superior position, androgyny, male-male and female-female sex, bondage, **fetishism**, and cross-dressing. At the end of the video/song, Madonna runs down the hall of the hotel giggling, with an expression of delight and mischief on her face about her own "shocking" imagination. The picture fades to the words "Poor is the man whose pleasures depend on the permission of another."

In this video fantasy, Madonna undoes the dominant discourse's forcible linking of desire, identity, and practice by presenting a couple whose "identity" does not seem at all ambiguous (hetero man/woman), who engage in practices where hetero intercourse is just one among many pleasures, whose desires are not genitally directed but focused, more than anything perhaps, on the gaze (the pleasure par excellence of video art). The erotic here privileges gender indeterminacy and the indeterminacy of the love object as well. Fetishism is eroticized, as is transvestism, so that it is not the body as a reified and fixed identity that is celebrated, but bodies as conditions of possibility for multiple pleasures. Furthermore, the repressive regime of Catholicism is incorporated in the fantasy to lend it the thrill of erotic transgression, as well as to point to the fact that Catholicism is indeed an erotic theology by its very incarnational nature, its focus on the flesh as a site of both pain and ecstasy.

One might argue that the video is nothing more than a sophisticated version of sexual tourism (Jack and Jill visit the world of sexual kinkiness), but that would be to ignore the frame and context of the narrative, an erotic reverie by one person. This is a fantasy about bodies and pleasures, a fantasy that suggests that the erotic need not be linked to genital sexuality, need not be linked to actual acts at all, and need not confine anyone to fixed identities or roles. It even suggests that straight people could go a long way toward complicating their notions of the erotic, the way that gays and lesbians have perforce already done. Finally, Madonna (as usual) places the female protagonist in the position of supreme control: she is the top in the scenes, the one who orders and directs them, the one who, indeed, creates them. Thus she helps break down the dominant culture's notion that straight women are the passive recipients of male desire and argues for women's sexual agency and choice as well. I still have trouble with the quotation at the end: "Poor is the man whose pleasures depend on the permission of another." I know that what is meant is that pleasure can reside in the domain of fantasy and does not need to be restricted and regulated by a reproductive heterosexual economy, but the phrase has the potential to suggest that consent in matters of sexuality should not be of concern.

The quotation's ambiguity points to one of the most difficult challenges for radical pluralists and sex radicals in coalition building during this time of publicly staged oppositions to the regime of moral absolutist antisex campaigns. That is, of course, a certain feminist dilemma or skepticism about discourses that promote sexual liberation without regard for the danger that the heterosexual regime of male sexuality historically and actually presents. This is where Jeffrey Weeks's insistence on the importance of choice, relationship, context, and meaning becomes crucial (*Sexuality and Its Discontents*, 218). These criteria can be usefully applied to representation as much as to other kinds of events or acts. Solidarity with those who experience sexuality as a danger or a threat will be crucial for the formation of successful sexual liberation movements that have as their goal the liberation of people from sexual violence as well as the liberation of people's erotic choices.

Another Madonna performance that presents a similar challenge through the vehicle of autoeroticism, fantasy, and "sensible" sex is the third remake of her song "Like a Virgin" from the Blonde Ambition tour (1990). The video is also about female agency in that it is about a woman masturbating, manipulating her own fantasy to produce pleasure for herself. The I/you of the song "Like a Virgin" thus becomes a joke: it is about a woman talking to herself. It specifically addresses the issue of female sexual agency by redesignating body parts so that the reign of the **phallus** is undermined. But instead of communicating the message that a phallus is really just a penis and a penis is for pleasure, Madonna "phallicizes" other body parts, specifically the breasts. Through this video performance she redesignates breasts as powerful erotic objects akin to what the dominant culture usually ascribes to heterosexual male sexuality, the all-powerful phallus/penis as embodiment of power. The camera focuses on her crotch and breast as places from which power and seduction emanate; our gaze is directed and guided toward her crotch, as though "there were something there"; this is the filmic equivalent of Madonna's other famous ironic gesture of crotch grabbing.[19] In another joke about breasts and penises, the "eunuchs" in attendance signal the absence of phallic power through a displacement of the male member to the breasts. The breasted men act both as mirrors of Madonna's actions and as her "sexual servants" in the scene. Their gender is deliberately "bent" so that at one point a breast behaves like a phallic object by being thrust between Madonna's legs, while at another point the man to the right of Madonna caresses his prosthetic breast. Likewise, Madonna's breasts are covered with a hard conical shell and made to look prosthetic. Finally, the men themselves are clothed so that their entire bodies seem to resemble a penis.

The video addresses First World erotic fantasies about the Third World, here in its most familiar nineteenth-century form, **orientalism**.[20] The image of the exoticized Middle Eastern harem is restaged with several ironic twists. In the context of the concert narrative, Madonna is staging the Annunciation phase of the life of the Virgin Mary. The song ends with "God?" as a question and a writhing sequence of Madonna holding her stomach, then, of course, she sings "Like a Prayer." In doing this, Madonna combines the story of the Virgin with the story of another Mary, Mary Magdalene, the whore. The lyrics to the song can be interchangeably applied to both. In this context, the Middle Eastern setting makes sense, as does the brothel-like atmosphere of the decor. The two men, like the dancer in "Justify My Love," function as spiritual, magical elements as—dare I say it?—angels or Holy Ghosts.

So the Annunciation or "virgin birth" is reinterpreted as an extravagant erotic fantasy to accompany masturbation. I say fantasy, and repeat that the men are supposed to be magical or spiritual in some sense, because at the moment when Madonna gets serious about her masturbation, they disappear, as though to signal that they belong to a different visualized dimension of the scene. One could say their breasts also confirm this, that they are fantasmatic images of androgynous erotic beings who simultaneously mirror the protagonist and pleasure her.

Perhaps the most disturbing aspect of the performance is its inscription of the colonial relation, Third World men "emasculated" and made to serve the erotic fantasies of the ultra First World woman. I would like to argue that this is a **postcolonial** representation that carries with it an ironic awareness of its orientalism. Given that it is a fantasy, and that the men, whatever else one might say about them, are not denied agency, I would suggest that this is a self-conscious representation of a First World erotic fantasy that confines itself to just that—a fantasy—for it is a scene of masturbation, a scene of one. Finally it resists appropriation into the norm of First World heterosexual fantasy about the Third World precisely because it adds the prosthetic breasts, a marker of "another gender," and because of the costumes and bodies of the men, which elide the masculine markers that would serve the First World female heterosexual fantasy. It is reasonable also, I think, to argue that it does not fit into the fantasy discourse of the First World heterosexual man. The final argument I would make about its irony is the gesture, repeated twice in the performance, of the three joining hands (slapping five) to the words "When your heart beats next to mine." This, it seems to me, is a conspiratorial gesture, a signal that the performance is an insider's joke.

Nevertheless, neither Madonna nor any First World popular culture is immune to or can completely resist the eroticization of the Third World and the imperialism that, in part, has produced such eroticization. It cannot simply be argued that fantasies are "harmless" by virtue of being fantasies. In a world where such imperialism had been undone, in a world where racism had been dismantled, we might argue that the racial/gender differences in this performance are "merely" erotic because, as Mary Douglas points out, mixed categories are generally taboo, and what is taboo is often eroticized (*Purity and Danger*). But in this world and with this history, the scene seems overdetermined, sedimented with the politics that make it an all-too-familiar imperialist scenario. If it is ironic, then perhaps it points to a way out of the dilemmas presented most acutely in the debates around sadomasochism as reenactments of political domination and subordination.[21] The fantasies are there; live them in the masturbatory domain of the bedroom; and finally, bring them out and place them on a stage, hold up a mirror to the culture, make of these fantasies an arena of the social where they can be critiqued and contested.[22]

D. *Truth or Dare*

It is not enough to interpret Madonna as a text, to give a close reading that, in some way or another, "canonizes" her as the postmodern diva of popular culture. This is the reaction of many enthusiasts. If we want to practice cultural reading, it is also important to perform what Wallace calls an "institutional, theoretical, and political critique" ("Negative Images," 656), and this analysis will include, in Madonna's case, asking questions about gender, race, and sexuality. This is why I think she is a good choice of an object to analyze. She introduces these questions forcefully into the cultural arena, the arena of cultural production and critique. Her work invites us aggressively to ask questions about the construction and deployment of gender, race, and sexuality.

Partly in relation to her own very controversial 1979 book that was denounced by June Jordan, *Black Macho and the Myth of the Superwoman*, Wallace finds it more significant that cultural productions by Black women exist than that they be located firmly on only one or the other side of an ideological divide (*Invisibility Blues*, 654–57).[23] As she points out, the "silence" of Black women's voices in cultural representations produces a situation where Black women can be either daytime or nighttime Oprah: Oprah of the *Oprah Winfrey Show* or Mattie on *The Women of Brewster Place*. Further, what is displayed (or concealed) by these representations is the ideological presupposition that any Black woman may freely choose to follow one example or the other. This is an example of individualism and the notion of "freedom to choose," whereas a critique that includes political, social, economic, and historical dimensions dismantles a simplistic notion of choice and reveals the conditions that determine and overdetermine both of these stereotypes.

I would contend that this sort of situation is still at work in our culture for white women as well. I want to discourage an analysis of

Madonna that assumes that any individual woman is completely free to choose from among any number of equally available representational choices and exploit any one of them, that those choices are freely made, and that therefore each individual is responsible as an individual for the choices s/he makes in terms of how s/he will be represented in the culture. What are the options for white women in representational terms? And what are the ideological presuppositions involved? One very familiar set of representational options is the virgin/whore option, the good girl/bad girl dichotomy.

We might also argue that in the world of popular music production, there is the artist/mannequin option, the classic division between pop and rock. Women almost always get located on the pop side as the mannequins, that is, the noncreative, noncontrolling non-artists who have only a voice (here voice itself becomes the ironic figure for a kind of silence, since the female vocalist is seen to be ventriloquizing the artistic genius of a no doubt male artist/producer).[24] Using a racial articulation of these terms, we might think about the classic racist division for the music industry: R&B (rhythm and blues) versus pop or mainstream. There are separate charts of popularity, one traditionally Black and one traditionally white. "Crossover" has been used to describe Black artists who make it onto the white charts. Recently stars such as George Michael and Madonna have aspired to the position of reverse crossover, making it on the Black charts as well as the white ones, through their deliberate and highly self-conscious use of R&B.

bell hooks continues to fall prey to the individualist myth about some cultural representations, while deploying different standards for others.[25] Thus she writes of Madonna as though Madonna should have been some kind of political revolutionary. Instead of furthering the cause (of white women? of gays? of people of color?), Madonna is accused of harming the people she is seen as representing. But it is important to think about how Madonna's deployment of sexual, racial, and gender categories fits into the context of such cultural representations and comments on them, in ways that uncover, articulate, and analyze the contradictions and complexities at work. One might ask the question, if you are white, why feature artists of color in your work at all? There are plenty of pop stars who do not. hooks wants it both ways when she says, "Certainly her expressed affinity with black culture enhances her value" (162). Why should this be true? If in fact, racism devalues African Americans and their cultural productions, why would it necessarily enhance Madonna's value to express her affinity with Black culture? Perhaps one answer to this question might be that African American musical cultural production represents a kind of authenticity, an authenticity that any white female pop star would desperately need as part of her image in order to be taken seriously as an artist.[26]

Like any star, a white woman trying to succeed in the pop music industry faces certain dilemmas in the culture, dilemmas of how to accrue power and agency, how to be viewed as in control and in charge. One of the reasons for Madonna's representational positioning among (originally) young boys, then among gay men of color, or, as in "Like a Prayer," among Black communities and Black men and women, is that she wants to accrue a certain power or authority. In other words, these are groups that white women still look more powerful in comparison to, and Madonna is always attempting to construct herself as powerful.

This sounds cynical and every bit as exploitative as hooks suggests, but it is important to see this in context, as one of the few alternatives available for constructing the white-woman-as-powerful image. What mitigates its oppressive nature is the simultaneous construction of marginality as Madonna's position: her self-construction as lower-middle-class, inauthentic, superficial, her self-construction as sexual outlaw, bad girl, not a good singer, not a great dancer, and a motherless child. So Madonna locates herself at the center of the margins. hooks's perspective tends to place Madonna too much at the center of the center, as though she were a Donald Trump or Bruce Springsteen. If we want to find parallels to Madonna's self-construction and success as pop culture superstar, we might want to look at the careers of people like Michael Jackson, George Michael, or, most recently, Whitney Houston. Houston's case is really interesting because it represents a complex visual/ideological representational construction of a Black woman in relation to white men. We might want to say that just as, according to hooks, Black women are completely elided in Madonna's racial text, so too white women are completely elided in Whitney Houston's racial text. We need to consider the complex and inter-structured interactions of both gender and race in cultural construc-tions. Why does the visibility of a woman depend somehow on the erasure of other women in these cultural scenes?

Madonna's deployment of sexuality complicates the race/gender script, as I mentioned. We might want to argue that the invisibility of Black women in the book *Sex* demonstrates the extent to which the book itself is not without conservative dimensions. Whereas almost every sexual positioning gets represented in Madonna's work (white gay men, S/M, gay men of color, hetero Black men, hetero Black women, white lesbians, etc.), there are no lesbians of color in her rep-resentations. This, I think, is the political threshold of Madonna's cul-tural representations, and it is no surprise that bell hooks writes in protest as a Black woman. What seems so problematic here is the bonding between women who are differently positioned racially. My article ("Our Lady of MTV") describes what happens between "Like a Prayer" and the Pepsi television commercial featuring Madonna singing the same song with different visuals, and points to one way the problem of the erasure of the other woman gets figured; ironically, voice functions to erase the body of the Black woman, so that she is not voiceless but bodiless.[27]

Finally, hooks does not consider the material dimensions of Ma-donna's relationship to race, only the representational dimensions. While she does indeed situate these representations in the context of a web of social and political institutions, she does not look at the indus-try or labor aspects of what Madonna is doing. It is true, however one wants to look at it, that, for *Truth or Dare* at least, Madonna assisted the dancing, singing, and acting careers of her performance troupe. The relationship is a kind of "matronage," a relationship whereby the boss's employees do not remain invisible, contributing their labor only to the profit of the boss/capitalist. Madonna's use of these specific dancers contributes to their careers, a fact of which they are well aware. This is an important dimension of the politics of cultural pro-duction that must be analyzed along with representational politics. Madonna is probably one of the relatively few white women in a position to enable the less empowered subjects she represents in her cultural productions to attain for themselves the level of cultural producer.

Truth or Dare deploys a familiar metaphor for white female empowerment and gives it a different meaning, a meaning that produces Madonna as businesswoman, artistic genius, hard worker, star, in charge, in control, not just in the private sphere of the family but in the public world. And it tries to refigure the powerful woman in charge in a way that does not completely demonize her. Powerful and important white women in this culture are usually represented as vicious, aggressive viragoes: cold, heartless, unfeminine, greedy, unnatural, and denatured. The metaphor deployed in *Truth or Dare* is, rather, the maternal metaphor: Madonna as mother. This is a metaphor that moves throughout Madonna's cultural production: in her name, of course, in her necessary self-mothering (because her mother is dead), in several of her videos, in her self-construction as powerful, in her assertion of "pussy power," and in the title of her song about cunnilingus on the album *Erotica:* "Where Life Begins."

Truth or Dare is thus a strategic deployment of matriarchal family fictions. Madonna's self-construction as "mother" to her "children" in the film takes up the context of the houses within New York City's ball circuit. José Gutierrez and Luis Camacho are both "children" of the House of Extravaganza (there is a relation here between this film and Jennie Livingston's *Paris Is Burning*, which treats the same subject in a more "authentically" ethnographic fashion; hooks also, by the way, dislikes this latter film). Madonna, then, plays the role of Pepper Labeija in *Paris Is Burning*. Another way the maternal script functions is that when Madonna goes to her mother's grave, it is framed in the film by her loss of voice; in one of her songs, "Oh Father," she has an incredibly disturbing image of her mother's wake, where we see the mother laid out in her coffin with her lips sewn shut. Thus Madonna somehow connects silencing and voicelessness to the mother, and her own self-mothering gets figured as giving voice. Madonna's maternalism is political, aesthetic, personal, and pragmatic: it serves to bind together a complexly articulated performative troupe for the duration of a concert tour. José and Luis, in an interview in *NYQ,* also describe her as their mother, and Oliver, Kevin, and Gabriel, who brought a suit against Madonna for profits from the film, describe their feeling of betrayal in familial terms, saying that they thought she was their mother and would take care of them.[28]

"Maternalism" is thus a pragmatic fiction for Madonna, a means of exercising power while defending herself from some of the charges of monstrosity directed at the white woman who takes too much control. It "domesticates" the power relations (relations that are primarily economic) in which she is involved. She thus represents herself as a denying/nurturing mother rather than an exploitative capitalist boss. She also demonstrated this pragmatic matronage when she signed José and Luis onto her recording company, Maverick, a corporation that is designed to scout unknown talent, to sponsor, produce, and distribute the work of new artists. Thus we have an example of how female self-construction as corporate mogul uses the maternal metaphor.[29] I think it is easy to see why a woman like Madonna would use the maternal metaphor to construct her economic power and her corporate identity as a tough, disciplined mom. But no single aspect of this maternalism can be ignored in this construction; for Madonna, the personal dimension seems just as important in the fictional persona she constructs.[30]

hooks further argues that Madonna deploys stereotypical notions of Black masculinity. This reveals how important it is to take sexuality into account in analyzing a given representation, the level of its appropriation, and its effects. Madonna uses primarily gay men of color in her film and videos. Black gay masculinity is coded differently than heterosexual Black masculinity, and I would venture that no one watching the film makes the mistake of confusing the two. Madonna may play off of the stereotypes about Black heterosexual masculinity, but the joke is precisely that we are talking about a very differently constructed masculine sexuality (here I am thinking of the scene where Madonna is in bed with her performers and makes a joke about Black penis size). Finally, in relation to the question of gay sexuality, it would also be possible to argue that one configuration that Madonna is deploying is the **fag hag** theme, that she is parodying the fag hag role, where instead of the woman being the kind of ignored, devalued sidekick of the gay men, you have Madonna as sidekick, Madonna as fag hag: a parody, because in this case Madonna claims most of the attention. This interacts complexly with some of the other effects of racial and sexual difference in the film, but in any case, it is clear that each dimension (racial, sexual, gender, class) of the identity categories explored is to be carefully read for the way it means "differently" in combination with the other dimensions.[31]

| F O U R |

Identity Politics
and Postcoloniality

A. Race and Identity Politics

In the preceding chapter I demonstrated some of the ways popular culture represents sexuality and sexual subcultures and the racialization of bodies and sexualities. Here I want to explore cultural productions that attempt in some way or another to reconfigure the terms of racial, sexual, and gender identity, conflict, and community in the United States. We have seen how Madonna's work complexly interweaves these issues. *Paris Is Burning* (Livingston, 1990), which I will discuss below, also raises issues of the intersections of racial identity, sexuality, and gender. Before doing this, however, I will sketch some of the issues and definitions involved in two political phenomena, one national and one international, that centrally engage questions of racial and national domination and that inform current popular culture and its theorizations in the United States: identity politics and postcoloniality.

The cultural productions examined here all engage in some form of polemic against the dominant culture. "Race," understood primarily as Black and white difference, structures the **imaginary** of the United States in particular ways. The history of the disenfranchisement of African Americans and their struggles for enfranchisement is in many ways constitutive of the self-understanding of the United States, even when it is not recognized as such. This structuring conflict takes specific forms in the United States, and is differently configured in representations of racial conflict elsewhere; in Homi Bhabha's and Kobena Mercer's discussions of England in *Cultural Studies*, "race" is understood and analyzed in relation to a colonial history.[1] hooks uses the term "decolonizing the mind" to talk about resistance to internalized racism, but the use of "colonialism" to describe U.S. white domination of African Americans is more metaphorical than literal, and British cultural productions help to articulate some of those differences.[2]

Identity politics—struggles to resist domination on the basis of constructed identities—takes as its model in the United States the civil rights movements of the fifties and sixties, as well as the Black Power movement and Black nationalism. Most identity politics movements define themselves in comparison with Black struggles: either the struggle is considered similar to the political struggles of African Americans, or it is defined as different from those struggles. At various times, the women's movement in the United States has used the metaphor of white domination of African Americans in order to explain its own struggle, and the debate about discrimination against gays in the military draws upon the comparison to the political struggles for racial desegregation of the military. Thus, in some sense, it is no surprise that Black, the racial designation, comes to stand in for "difference" as such. One of the problems that sometimes arises in these comparisons is that an identity is never singular. Issues of race, sexuality, and gender intersect; they are intimately interwoven and cannot be separated into separate bodies. Bodies are racially and sexually marked, and they are gendered too.

In the eighties and nineties, identity politics has focused on this intersectionality, and popular culture seems to be grappling with ways of representing the multidimensional aspects of identities, or subject positions. As Marlon Riggs points out in his film about Black gay male identity, *Tongues Untied* (1994), it is absurd to ask, "Are you Black or are you gay?" because both are fundamental and inseparable components of a person's identity and experience. Even the institutionalized forms of political struggle around identity politics, such as multiculturalism and what has come to be called political correctness (PC), recognize some of the complexities of reducing identity to a singular notion of what a body and its social meanings are.[3]

Identity as a concept is shaped by the European American bourgeois political tradition that is embodied in our legal system, our constitution, and our political institutions. Identity politics, as struggles to resist racism, homophobia, and sexism, take up what is initially an identity imposed on people as one of the forms of domination. In other words, it is the dominators who first confer an identity on the dominated, in political terms, and that identity is a negative one; Black, gay, woman are initially defined in negative terms by the dominators. The people designated by these terms then take them up, appropriate them for their own uses and definitions, invert the binary, reclaim the identity in question, and polemically redefine it in positive terms, thus using those originally negative identities as the basis for reclaiming rights as equals in the polity.[4]

But as with the inversion of other **binary oppositions**, certain problems emerge: the reclaiming of the negative identity as a positive one does not necessarily undo the logic of binary opposition, and it elides the differences that may exist within each of the terms. The logic of binary opposition presumes that each term—Black and white, for example—is internally consistent and coherent, rather than containing a difference within. This is why, I think, it is so hard for identity politics movements to arrive at analyses and politics that take into account all aspects of a person's oppression, and the ways different forms of oppression affect each other and inscribe themselves on one and the same body. Thus hooks and Angie Chabram-Dernersesian both critique the masculinism of the Black Power and Chicano liberation movements, while hooks also critiques the whiteness of feminism, and Riggs critiques the heterosexism of Black nationalism. Queer politics has recently attempted to subvert the terms of binary definitions and binary oppositions to arrive at a more successful politics that more accurately or carefully analyzes its constituency, without excluding allies and without falling into some of the traps of exclusion and oppression that the concentration on only one identity often produces. The nueva Chicana politics together with the notion of *mestizaje* that Sandra Cisneros, Gloria Anzaldúa, Cherríe Moraga, and Angie Chabram-Dernersesian describe also subvert this binary by reclaiming hybridity (a non-identity, a mixed-ness) as a term of collective struggle.[5]

| 61 |

While it is logical and has often been politically useful to organize around an identity category, it continues to produce oppressions and exclusions that ultimately undermine the struggles that are conducted in the name of those identities. Thus many movements in the eighties and nineties have foregrounded the term "coalition politics," the idea of different identity groups coming together to organize around common goals. Let the politics configure the organizing, June Jordan argues; here the attempt is to organize around political categories: categories of struggle rather than identity categories.[6] Nevertheless, as with the concept queer, some inversion is clearly necessary; in other words, the oppressed identity must somehow constitute the point from which the definition emerges, just as queer, as a definition, emerges from gay, not straight. This initial inversion, whereby the previously devalorized and decentered term is valorized and centered, helps to avoid the traditional traps of antisexist and antiracist politics, where, ironically, people in the dominant identity categories have often continued to occupy leadership positions.

The struggles of identity politics are relevant because they are also conducted on the terrain of popular culture. hooks expresses her anger at Madonna's appropriations of Black culture for her own profit, and at Jennie Livingston's transformation of ritual into spectacle and the uncriticized celebration of whiteness that *Paris Is Burning* allows to be expressed.[7] In part, the urgency of her critique stems from an economy of scarcity in the arena of representation: if people of color do not have equal access to cultural production on a mass media scale, then representation is always a representation by the other, a "speaking for someone else," a ventriloquizing that silences those represented. One might argue that this is why Livingston does not speak in the film, in order not to overwhelm her subjects with her white authorial voice. On the other hand, it is clear that the film is constructed, even though the genre of documentary often produces the illusion of "you are there," the illusion, in other words, of a transparent reality; thus, regardless of its unmediated appearance, it too is in some sense a fiction that does not purport to accurately "represent" its subjects. This film draws attention to its constructedness by the inclusion of words on the screen that serve as a glossary or encyclopedia of slang terms. On the other hand, this same technique also performs a kind of anthropology of the natives for the (white) spectators in the metropolis; in other words, it explains to us, the outsiders, the rituals, language, and secrets of the insider group, and thus exposes the people constructed as "**other**," "native," "foreign," and "exotic" to us.

hooks rightly points out that we need to be aware of the politics that undergirds any commodification of Blackness in this society. And it is important to apply this to all dominated and exoticized groups in the culture. It is also important to realize that the identity of the cultural producer will not necessarily guarantee the production of "good" representations. **Commodity culture** has its own logic, and commodified representations will partake of the politics of consumer capitalism. It is thus important to critique notions of authenticity, purity, truth, and accuracy in relation to these considerations.

"Authenticity" and "experience" are frequently invoked to provide a valid foundation for identity politics. Identity as such does not automatically guarantee a certain body of experience, and experience does not automatically attach itself to an identity. Thus Vanilla Ice may have more in common, culturally, with Public Enemy than does Clarence Thomas, to exaggerate a little. And Madonna may have more in common with African American Catholics in Detroit than bell hooks does. Jennie Livingston too, by virtue of having been a New York City lesbian, may (although not necessarily) have more in common with her subjects than bell hooks does, as a working-class heterosexual woman from the South. That is why I think it is important to ask questions about the complexities of these representations. If we agree with hooks's feeling that, for instance, Madonna's relation to her subjects is exploitative, then we need to be careful and specific about why.

This issue also arises in relation to the question of whether an "insider" or an "outsider" is responsible for the representation in question.[8] The commonsense notion (and this comes up in hooks's interrogation of *Paris Is Burning*) is that an outsider's representation will be a misrepresentation, that is, it will be inaccurate and distorted, whereas an insider's representation will be true and accurate. But is any one representation the truth? The criteria of accuracy and truth cannot help us discern the difference between insiders' and outsiders' points of view. We need to think in more complex ways about this question. To assume automatically that an outsider's point of view is inaccurate or wrong is to buy into the notion of oneself as the privileged analyst of one's own culture, and the notion that culture is something that no one "outside" it can understand. Yet no one person is a privileged carrier of the truth of his or her culture, because, in part, culture is not something that can be located in an individual. Culture, by definition, involves a disparate group of loosely interrelated people and their ways of life.

hooks argues that Livingston does not display a sufficient awareness of the socioeconomic and political conditions that determine the lives of the queens represented by the film. Observations like this can help us think about the ambiguous politics of representation in a **dialectical** way, even when such observations do not seem dialectical enough. In other words, they may prompt us to ask questions about which aspects of the representation in question are politically productive, which are politically problematic, and how they interact. It may be that we will always have to say, "on the one hand, . . . on the other hand, . . ." without being able to come to a conclusion about the politics of a given representation. Contestation, such as that performed by hooks, is always useful in that it produces debate and argument in the public arena, and this debate is one of the ways we refine and redefine how we think about the conflicts and issues that are represented by popular culture, and how these conflicts and issues play themselves out in the culture.

For example, one of the things one might want also to critique about *Paris Is Burning* is its gender politics: does it subvert or uphold traditional notions of femininity and desirability? How? What about the elision of "biological" women in the film, when it is clear that they occupy a space in the arena of the balls as support workers? Perhaps Livingston's gay identification here, which helps to foreground the strength, beauty, and creative agency of queens, also serves in some ways to cover over or deny other elements of the sociocultural configuration she represents, for example, the ways traditional notions of female beauty continue to be bolstered by the film, or the ways the real support and service labor of women is erased. The ending of the film, in particular, seems problematic with regard to the issue of gender. We see that Willie Ninja, the most masculine dancer, performer, and

queen, rises to phenomenal success, while the more traditionally feminine queens, the pre-operative **transsexuals**, either come to a tragic
and unhappy end, like Venus, or are never heard from again, like Octavia. What is this film saying about gender then?[9]

Finally, hooks's essay "Is Paris Burning?" illustrates some of the reasons that we must ask all the relevant questions of identity and subject
positioning when analyzing such a representation. While her essay focuses carefully on the political complexities of a white woman's representation of impoverished African American and Latino men, it does
not equally take into account the political complexities of their gay
identities and, further, the ways "drag" or cross-dressing function not
as pure "play," but as a dimension of identity that is about constraints
and endangerments as well. In the opening passage of the essay, she
quotes her journal entry about herself and her boyfriend disguising
themselves, dressing in drag and going out as boys together. She
frames her journal entry with the following commentary:

> There was a time in my life when I liked to dress ᴜp as a male and go
> out into the world. It was a form of ritual, of play. It was also about
> power. To cross-dress as a woman in patriarchy—then, more so than
> now—was also to symbolically cross from the world of powerlessness
> into a world of privilege. It was the ultimate, intimate, voyeuristic ges-
> ture. . . . Cross-dressing, appearing in drag, transvestism, and transsexu-
> alism emerge in a context where the notion of subjectivity is challenged,
> where identity is always perceived as capable of construction, invention,
> change. (145)

What disappears in this passage is the very real danger that a queen
faces in mainstream society, or that gays and lesbians who perform
cross-gender identification face on the streets. What hooks portrays
here is a benign world where the worst that can happen when you
dress up and go out in drag is that people will laugh. In other words,
she does not imagine the renunciation of her heterosexual identity and
the privilege to "pretend" that comes with it, as she exposes herself
disguised in the culture. Finally, the passage also assumes that the desire to change one's identity and/or subjectivity occurs in a context
where such change is imagined as possible; accounts of gender dysphoria such as Leslie Feinberg's *Stone Butch Blues* or testimonials by

transsexuals reveal a far more agonistic framework for this desire and document the brutalities involved in the "choice" to change.

B. Postcoloniality, Imperialism, Third World: Background and Context

The work of cultural producers in the United States can be contextualized within a broader, international framework of resistance struggles. Many of the U.S. identity politics movements emerged from and, in turn, influenced international struggles for the liberation of oppressed people from regimes of domination. The term "Third World" has come to designate a loose sense of alliance among people of color in such struggles worldwide. In the preface to *Third World Women and the Politics of Feminism*, the editors write,

> While the term *third world* is a much maligned and contested one, we use it deliberately, preferring it to *postcolonial* or *developing* countries. *Third World* refers to the colonized, neocolonized, or decolonized countries (of Asia, Latin America, Africa) whose economic and political structures have been deformed within the colonial process, and to black, Asian, Latino, and indigenous peoples in North America, Europe, and Australia. Thus the term does not merely indicate a hierarchical cultural and economic relationship between "first" and "third" world countries; it intentionally foregrounds a history of colonization and contemporary relationships of structural dominance between first and third world peoples. In drawing on histories of antiracist, antiimperialist struggles around the world, the term *third world* is also a form of self-empowerment. However, the unproblematized use of a term such as *third world women* could suggest the equation of struggles and experiences of different groups of women, thus flattening and depoliticizing all internal hierarchies. The term could also suggest that "third" world cultures or "ethnicity" is the primary or only basis of the politics of third world women. We intend neither.[10]

As the above quotation suggests, the term is highly contested; since it is used to designate a category of politically interventionist cultural production by people of color, in the United States and elsewhere, I wish to explore the way it can be seen to broaden identity politics to include the history of European imperialism and colonialism. While many of the representations previously discussed address the domestic policies of the nation-state, the invocation of Third World brings global relations of dominance into focus.

Third World immediately suggests other key terms and concepts, such as imperialism, colonialism, nationalism, domination, nation-state, citizenship, racism, and sexism, but also decolonization (national liberation struggles), resistance, opposition, agency, and subjectivity. These might all be collocated under the heading of "relations of ruling."[11] Colonialism implies an occupying force that settles in annexed territory, the installation of a settler colony consequent upon imperialist invasion and annexation that then transforms the invaded country—colonizes it—by forcing it into economic, social, and political dependency on the metropolis, or the center of rule within the invading nation-state. The most familiar reference for the description of imperialism and colonization is Europe in the nineteenth century, the empire-building economic and political ventures of England, France, and Portugal. But one could also argue that colonization describes the history of the United States' dispossession of the indigenous inhabitants of North America, and there is some support for claiming that Puerto Rico and Hawaii occupy the position of current-day colonies of the United States.

The influential recent period of decolonization for Third World movements and for U.S. identity politics was the sixties. In her analysis of the recent history of the Third World, Barbara Harlow calls this a crucial period for resistance literature.[12] The term "Third World" was coined at the Bandung Conference in 1955 to name the then nonaligned nations. The initial phase of the struggle lasted from 1954, when Vietnam claimed victory over the French, to Algerian independence in 1962. There followed a period of success for national liberation movements: from the Cuban revolution in 1959 to the fall of Saigon in 1975 (this period saw the liberation of Nigeria in 1960; Kenya in 1973; Guinea-Bissau in 1974; and Mozambique and Angola in 1975) (Harlow, 5–6).

One might, of course, argue that all nation-states are formed through imperialist expansion. Imperialism is related to the word empire/*imperium*: a nation-state aspires to acquire additional territory and annex it to its own. Imperialism can take place on different levels and usually involves territorial annexation, economic and political annexation, juridical (legal) annexation, and ultimately ideological and cultural annexation; these latter are often referred to as **cultural imperialism,** a phenomenon that acquires central importance in Third World cultural production. Harlow discusses cultural or mental decolonization as a "literature/criticism that is participatory in the historical processes of hegemony and resistance to domination rather than (only) formal and analytic" (9–10). Collective and concerted resistance to programmatic cultural imperialism thus comes to be called "cultural" or "mental" decolonization.

These terms are used in their metaphorical as well as their literal senses, so that there is imperialism, strictly speaking, as well as something called cultural imperialism, or decolonization, and something hooks calls "decolonizing the mind" (*Yearning,* 5). It is useful to employ these terms both literally and metaphorically, but there are pitfalls as well. For example, to use the term "colonizing" in its metaphorical sense (as in "colonizing the mind" or "decolonizing the mind") risks individualizing and personalizing the process, thus giving a false impression. Colonizing becomes something anyone can do, rather than a system that involves a nation with military-industrial resources to deploy. In other words, to use the term "colonization" in its metaphorical sense risks rendering it unsystematic and nonstructural, which can mislead one as to the nature and persistence of power. Furthermore, it elides the economic, political, and juridical dimensions of imperialism and colonization, which are all crucial mechanisms in the enforcement of relations of ruling, that is, domination.

Harlow contrasts resistance literature—the narrative cultural production of Third World postcolonial writers—with the tradition of the bourgeois novel emerging around the same time in Europe (the nineteenth century being considered the great age of the bourgeois novel) (114). The typical narrative she focuses on as an example of this tradition is the *bildungsroman,* the story of an individual's growing up, which focuses on the solitary nature of man, his existential dilemmas, and his relation to society as an extraneous force. For female protagonists this takes the form of the sentimental novel: the woman grows up, meets a man, encounters obstacles to love, resolves those problems, marries the man, and the story ends. Harlow identifies these narratives as expressions of a particular middle-class ideology: the idea is to grow up, get educated, acquire property and a family, and find one's place in society. But as many have pointed out, these novels can be read differently, in a way that focuses on social and historical context. Edward Said, for example, shows how the nineteenth-century European bourgeois novel does include anxious realizations of Europe's place in the global context.[13] Certainly there are also European novels that document the social upheavals brought on by the industrial revolution and its consequences for the working classes, but these too focus on the metropolis as the site of social unrest, rather than situating European economic and social transformations in a global context. Resistance literature, in Harlow's reading, assumes a different kind of world, a world where no one is an isolated individual, where individual actions have historical consequences, and where the political dimension of the text is always at issue. It focuses most often, in her reading, on national liberation movements and the Third World's relation to the European metropolis.

Postcolonial resistance literature and other kinds of oppositional cultural production tend to combine Western liberal political categories with understandings of decolonization struggles emerging from a more Marxist tradition of class struggle. Frantz Fanon has chronicled the ways national liberation movements share features with liberal bourgeois rights-based discourses (the tradition I discussed earlier that informs many identity politics movements).[14] Many of the resistance novels Harlow discusses take place within a tradition of Marxist discourses of class struggle on the one hand, and discourses of decolonization on the other. Class struggle assumes a collectivity and does not focus on individuals; decolonization also focuses on occupiers and occupied, colonizers and colonized, classes of structurally related people rather than individual agents. However, rights discourses have caused certain kinds of identity markers to emerge as categories of struggle: gender, race, and sexuality, for example. These are characteristics that were not well accounted for in traditional revolutionary Marxist discourses of struggle, yet they have emerged in contemporary resistance novels as important categories affecting people's conditions and the kinds of systematic and individual oppression people experience. Many resistance narratives, particularly those written in the post-decolonized period, focus on the multiple markers and the multiple conditions that make up a person's relation to the world. This is why there is often a tension between traditional revolutionary discourse and the discourses of feminism, race consciousness, and queer liberation, since the latter do in fact emerge from bourgeois political traditions that stress the importance of the individual. On the other hand, because many recent cultural productions are hybrid products of these traditions—a Marxist tradition of class struggle, a tradition of nationalist resistance to colonization, and bourgeois rights-based discourses—they often seem internally contradictory. Thus, while Spike Lee, whom I discuss in the next chapter, might successfully define "race" as a category of domination requiring collective class resistance, he might at the same time fail to recognize gender as such a category, and consign it instead to the domain of the personal.

Chandra Mohanty's essay "Under Western Eyes" discusses the role of theory in what she calls "discursive struggle," how domination and resistance to domination take place on the discursive level as well as on the level of wars and military occupation.[15] She demonstrates very well how a theoretical approach or method, such as deconstruction, can be enlisted politically. For example, we might ask the question, what happens when one takes the West as the primary referent for one's perspective on the Third World? Deconstruction's insights with regard to the logic of Western metaphysics can be used here to illustrate how some of the cultural producers and the texts they create subvert the dominant logical paradigm of binary opposition.

One deconstructive insight about Western thinking is that it is organized around an identity/difference opposition, where concepts can be lined up in a series of binary oppositions:

identity/difference

same/other

day/night

on/off

reason/madness

mind/body

being/nothingness

sun/moon

light/dark

human/animal

man/woman

me/you

rich/poor

city/country

good/bad

First World/Third World

This is a logic of opposition, a logic of difference. Although these op-positions appear to be equals (term *a* is defined in terms of term *b*; term *a* is what term *b* is not), term *a* is positively valorized, while term *b* is negatively valorized. What appears to be a horizontal opposition is, in fact, a vertical one, with the valorized positive term on top. However, as the initial deconstructive insight makes clear, all these positively valorized terms are defined exclusively in relation to the terms they devalorize. For example, we define a man in terms of what he is not: a woman or an animal. The positive term is thus relational, but **Western logocentric ideology**, or this logic of difference, attrib-utes positive content to term *a* and effaces, erases, or elides its depen-dence on term *b* for the very meaning of its existence. Part of the work of deconstruction, then, is to expose this logic and the fact that the positively valorized term is dependent on the negatively valorized term, to systematically show how this is true and what its conse-quences are, and, hence, to politicize the issue.[16] Working against this ideology does not, however, mean simply reversing the terms, because that keeps one within the logic of difference, and the logic of absolute difference is a logic of opposition, which is agonistic and produces—or at least implies—violent relations to the other.

Difference is a notion that has been recently valorized, and there-fore it seems useful to unpack the ways difference, according to the analysis above, potentially carries with it pernicious consequences, both for defining differences between and among people and for political organizing. I would like, therefore, to compare it as a concept to a notion of diversity.[17] Briefly, difference is always between two terms and implies a polarity in which one term is defined as the negation of the other. Diversity, on the other hand, can be between two terms, but also between *x* number of terms, and refers to a system in which there are no absolute oppositions (though there are contraries). This distinction helps explain how certain kinds of differential systems—sexual difference, for example, and all other such systems, for example, racial difference—are currently understood according to a logic of absolute difference, and suggests alternative perspectives through the model of diversity.[18] Colors are a helpful illustration. When you have two teams, for example, you create a system of difference: the Blue team versus the Green team. But in fact only one color, one term, is needed for the system to work, because if one is not on the Blue team, then by definition one is on the Green team. In a system of diversity, on the other hand, not-blue could mean green, but it could also mean fuchsia or chartreuse or lavender; diversity would include the bystanders, the spectators, the umpire perhaps, and a host of others not necessarily associated with one of the two teams in question.

The logic of absolute difference is the logic of colonial rule, the logic of racism, sexism, and most systems of oppression that oppose one group of people (or one way to be) to another. Its ideological consequence, no matter who is using it, is a system of oppositions that justifies—whether consciously or not—the degradation of one term and the elevation of another. Any political position, whether imperialist or resistive, is potentially subject to this logic. Thus discursive struggle, the struggle over political meaning on the level of signs, plays a role in working against systems of domination and dominant ideologies.

C. Octavia Butler's Xenogenesis

Octavia Butler's *Xenogenesis* trilogy (comprising *Dawn, Adulthood Rites,* and *Imago*) engages in such discursive struggle on an imaginative level, by combining slavery, miscegenation, and reproductive technologies in a narrative of resistance that reinterprets the American past as a situation of colonial domination. The novels thus combine the insights of domestic identity politics with those of postcoloniality to refigure the past of U.S. slavery and imagine a postnational and "post"-racialist future.[19] Butler's vision, like Jewelle Gomez's, is deliberately progressive; both are explicit attempts to deal with present-day problems of racism and sexism in the context of an alternative world. Butler's primary theme is xenophobia, the irrational fear of the stranger, the other, the one who is "foreign" to oneself. Butler re-creates a scene that makes us uncomfortably self-conscious about typical First World imperialist myths and fantasies about the Third World other as self-destructive, primitive, requiring assistance. She reverses, to some extent, the stereotypical position of First and Third World by making the aliens (those who are "other")—at least initially—figures for the First World imperialists and the humans (whom we would normally identify with) representative of the colonized.

Butler's vision, while it engages the dystopic discourse of humankind's self-destruction through technology and intra-species hatred, also provides a utopian vision of future possibilities for humans predicated on humanity's "becoming other" than itself (that is, mixing genetically, and irrevocably, with the "alien" Oankali). It thus also suggests that, through miscegenation (which might be thought of in this text as some kind of deep interracial connecting), a new kind of creature can come into existence to change, transform, and challenge the hatred, bigotry, and narrow-minded "nationalism" Butler sees as humanity's major problems. Eva Cherniavsky argues that Butler's exploration of genetic mutation performs a critique of whiteness, thus racializing it:

Butler's "post-Americanist" narrative thus situates the promise of the postnational subject in a rearticulation of whiteness, which is made visible, on the Oankali body, as the mark of a marked (non-white, or non-Oankali) corporeality. In other words, the posting of American national identity does not hinge . . . on an affiliation of the white subject with marginal or subaltern cultures that leaves white privilege intact but on a critical racialization of whiteness. ("Subaltern Studies," 109)

By reversing the terms of the binary opposition's hierarchy, Butler allows readers to imagine the "terror of whiteness" bell hooks describes as the constant consciousness of the Black imagination:

> Socialized to believe the fantasy, that whiteness represents goodness and all that is benign and non-threatening, many white people assume this is the way black people conceptualize whiteness. They do not imagine the way whiteness makes its presence felt in black life, most often as terrorizing imposition, a power that wounds, hurts, tortures, as a reality that disrupts the fantasy of whiteness as representing goodness. ("Representing Whiteness in the Black Imagination," 340–41)

Utopian political genres, such as science fiction and fantasy, as I mentioned in the case of *The Gilda Stories*, configure the future in terms of the present and the past. These texts are thus attempts to work out global solutions to problems in the present by mapping out an imaginary world.[20] They do this, in part, because the issues being addressed have as yet no theoretical solution, and thus the technique of what is known as modeling is used. The author generates a world in order to see how posited dilemmas unfold in some kind of "real time." These narratives recognize and seek to manage or resolve political, economic, and social dilemmas: utopia imagines a resolution, whereas dystopia focuses on the consequences. But, perforce, the materials for these worlds must come from either the past or the present, for there is nothing else available; this is why, often, these texts also seem to lack imagination about the worlds they develop; *Xenogenesis*, for example, still envisions a situation where reproductive sexuality is primarily biological and heterosexual, whereas *The Gilda Stories* preserves intact, even into the future, the national borders of North and South America.

Octavia Butler's trilogy represents an effort to combine identity politics and Third World discourses of decolonization to situate questions of "race" in a global context. Her work and that of Gomez might be said to fit Harlow's definition of resistance literature in that they force upon readers an awareness of the historical and political stakes of their vision and suggest, obliquely, a program of action for the present and the future. Furthermore, Butler and Gomez both demonstrate the limits of a logic of difference by setting up an opposition—human versus alien, vampire versus human—and then problematizing it. Like some of the texts I will discuss in the next chapter, they suggest that humanity's only hope for survival lies in an undoing of the logic of binaries. For Gomez, as I argued in chapter 3, the new category that defies oppositional logic is something called a vampire; for Butler, it is a post-human hybrid. In both cases, however, the being beyond oppositional difference can be imagined only through nonexistent categories; thus these texts suggest as well that "resolutions" to present social dilemmas are more easily worked out on the discursive level than in present-day political and social practice.

FIVE

Multiculturalism's Migrations

A. Diasporic Identities and Sandra Cisneros

In this chapter I explore new configurations of race and migration in the United States and the cultural styles that have come to be called **diasporic cultures**, groups of people defined in part by their relation of exile or "outsider" status within the nations in which they live (African Americans, Mexican Americans, Asian Americans, Native Americans). Diaspora refers originally to the exile of the Jews in the Hebrew Bible and, since, to exile from a homeland and a history of perpetual persecution and wandering. It has been subsequently taken up in a more metaphorical sense to describe exilic experience, even when the existence of an originary homeland is in question.

For African Americans and Afro-Caribbeans, the exile and wandering take place as a result of the slave trade. Mexican Americans combine a history of both conqueror and conquered. They are descendants of the indigenous people of Aztlán ("the unifying impulse of Aztlán—the imaginary geography claimed as the true site of Chicano subjectivity"), people exterminated and/or displaced by the conquerors (Aztecs, Mayans, etc.).[1] They are also the descendants of the Spanish *conquistadores*, African slaves, and those who are later caught on the border between Mexico and what will become the United States, whether it be Texas, Arizona, or California.

Thus Chicano/a cultural identity comes to embody the quintessence of the "new" notion of hybrid cultural identity or *mestizaje— mestiza/o* meaning "mixed." Like "queer," this term undoes a simple binary notion, this time of race, of dominator and dominated. Thus, if queerness is the sexual figure of hybridity, then *mestizaje* is the racial figure of such diasporic hybridity. This cultural identity is founded not on a notion of purity of heritage or origins, not on a notion of clearly defined borders, but on a notion akin to James Clifford's idea of "traveling cultures": loosely cohesive U.S./Mexican/Latin American/indigenous American cultures whose hybridity or mixed-ness produces a kind of patchwork out of which the various strands cannot be separated. A diasporic culture, then, is a kind of cultural identity that takes what is initially a liability, a loss, and turns it into a distinctive and culturally affirming identity that can celebrate "homelessness" as well as mourn it.

For Chicanos/as this becomes especially important, since there is a "neither one nor the other" quality to Chicano/a identity: neither Mexican nor American. This dilemma is familiar in the context of the recent "hyphenated American." I say "recent" because it seems now that Irish Americans, Italian Americans, and others are accepted as being simply Americans, and do not "ride on the hyphen" the way African Americans, Asian Americans, and Mexican Americans do, those people whose identities are still fundamentally tied—by society at large—to the modifying term that comes before "American."[2] This may be attributed to color-racism (chromaticism), and to the specificity of the ways different groups of people are racialized. Racialization is not necessarily about hierarchization, though it may be. An important aspect of racialization is that it is not uniform across all dominated races, but differential; for example, Jews are racialized differently from African Americans, Latinos, and so forth.

Angie Chabram-Dernersesian articulates some of the history of Chicano identity politics in the sixties, voiced in conjunction with the Black Power movement and the American Indian movement.[3] As with any oppositional cultural identity, the Chicano movement reclaimed a past that included the heroes of the Mexican Revolution (1910): Pancho Villa (in the north) and Emiliano Zapata (in the south); those who fought in some way against either aristocratic landowner domination, imperialist invasion, or repressive government, and did so in the name of the people (*la Raza*). As a cultural identity, it also embodies a metaphoric notion of nationhood, and thus participates in some of the rhetoric of nationalism that bell hooks identifies as Black nationalism.[4]

Like the Black nationalism that hooks critiques, the Chicano movement initially was a masculinist one: "Nationalism's preferred male subject is imbued with a masculine, patriarchal ideology that resists the apologetic sympathies ascribed to it by Chicano cultural practitioners seeking to erase male domination from the semantic orbit of machismo," asserts Chabram-Dernersesian (83). As Sandra Cisneros explores in "Eyes of Zapata" and elsewhere in her collection of stories *Woman Hollering Creek*, there is an erasure of women within the glorified history of Chicano struggle. Chabram-Dernersesian discusses the nueva Chicana movement and how it redeems the scorned feminine identity: the *Malinche*, a term of derision used to signify betrayal. The name comes from Malintzin or, as she was called by the Spanish, Doña Marina, the indigenous woman who assisted Cortés, translating for him and ultimately helping him conquer the people of South America (84). Malintzin was considered a *vendida*—someone who "sold out." This identity has been reclaimed by Chicanas, especially lesbian feminists, whose feminism is perceived as a form of sellout to the race. Malintzin or *la Malinche* has been reclaimed as originator-mother too, because she had children by Cortés. She is also the figure of the interpreter or translator, the embodiment of the notion of "traveling culture."[5]

Chabram-Dernersesian also makes the point that this "new" Chicana identity is not a singular thing, but an acceptance of the multiple and varied identities within the one unified notion of Chicana:

> This nueva Chicana is figured by multiple female subjects who are linked together by a common history of work and protest. Yet these female subjects are located with different roles that confirm their allegiance to the movement and they are spoken in multiple expressions of gender that simultaneously reference family relations and political commitments. This practice of representation celebrates the camaraderie between Chicanas/os and creates an intimate bond between these women and their public. (85)[6]

Cisneros makes clear, as well, that it is not necessary for women to choose between *la Malinche* (the whore) and *la Virgen de Guadalupe* (the Virgin), that both can be reclaimed. At the end of the book we read a chapter that "transcribes" prayers and thanks to the Virgin that people leave in the church; the text of Chayo (whose name is also Rosario), symbol of la nueva Chicana, weaves together her Indian, Mexican, American history and reclaims all her female ancestors, both Catholic (the sign of conquest) and Aztec (124–29). Cisneros's book demonstrates the multiplicity Chabram-Dernersesian describes, for there are many speaking voices in the text, some male, some female, some straight, some gay, some human and mortal, some supernatural. There is also the mixture of the ancient and the new, the traditional and the radically modern, the old and the young, the liberated and the not so liberated. Cisneros's work thus acts as a kind of poetic manifesto of the nueva Chicana, for it combines history and myth, past and present, young and old, women and men, anger, sorrow, and loss, but also solidarity, into a patchwork of voices and narratives, poems and fragments, and it does so in multiple languages.

The mix of languages is especially important for Cisneros's work and for other Chicana/o cultural productions, as a tangible linguistic and graphic sign of hybridity. Furthermore, *Woman Hollering Creek* condenses its polemic in a figure—*la Gritona*, or the hollering woman—which transforms the traditional legend of *la Llorona*, the weeping woman, into a figure of female liberation. Thus, the story "Woman Hollering Creek" features a wild, independent woman (possibly a lesbian) conducting a female "underground railroad" to rescue women from domestic abuse; she drives a truck (like a man, the story suggests) and shouts every time she crosses the creek.[7] Sandra Cisneros's *Woman Hollering Creek*, then, like Gomez's *Gilda Stories* and Butler's *Xenogenesis* trilogy, produces, from the point of view of the ethnically, racially, and sexually marginalized, an imaginative representation of theoretical alternatives to the logic of binary oppositions in the dominant culture.

Diasporic cultural production, in its oppositional or resistive form, also challenges traditional or canonical genres. One formal aspect of such production involves the idea that a single narrative line will not work to represent the world of the hybrid. Instead, stories are fragmented and juxtaposed; they combine the elements of linguistic, narrative, and generic mixing that one finds in Cisneros's work, so that somehow the nature of diaspora will be fairly represented. Finally, an important element of diasporic cultural production has to do with a knowledge of history: "resistance narratives" demand that their readers learn the histories and myths of the people and places being invoked. In this context, it is useful to mention the distinction Michele Wallace makes between History—the Euroamerican form of reason, rationality, the "truth" of the past—and myth, the denigrated term for the narratives of the past that belong to the colonized. In Cisneros and the cultural production of other diasporic people, myth is reclaimed as an important aspect of history; further, they demand contextual knowledge on the part of the reader, who has to understand historical context to understand what the author is trying to do.[8]

For a people struggling for a place in history, telling their history and making readers learn it become all-important. So, for example, if one does not know much about the Mexican Revolution or the history of the relations between California, Texas, Arizona, and Mexico, one is compelled to do the research to become an educated reader of Cisneros's *Woman Hollering Creek*. Once one begins to acquire the historical background, then the history that Cisneros adds to this—the legends and myths of the nameless hollering women who have left their marks but do not find a place in official histories—becomes what the reader discovers from the text. Thus Cisneros, in a gesture of Chicana feminist recovery, secures a place for these women in diasporic history.

B. *Do the Right Thing*

Discussions of oppositional texts and representations invoke questions of political responsibility and accountability to one's community. One debate that frequently occurs in public culture when such representations circulate is whether the author or director or producer of the representation is accountable to his or her community, understood to be those members of the group sharing the identity represented. hooks, for example, bases many of her judgments concerning popular culture on this criterion of accountability. This issue is related to the question of whether a given representation is "true" or accurate with regard to the people and subcultures it represents. What are the moral responsibilities of these cultural workers toward the subject matter they represent? Are cultural workers accountable to their communities? Why or why not? How does this differ from the traditional notion of artistic integrity and freedom? What makes oppositional subcultures engage in the question of accountability? Who feels this accountability, and who does not?

A good example of a cultural producer whose accountability to African Americans has been much debated is the director Spike Lee, because Lee is the best-known popular Black filmmaker in the United States today. hooks and Wallace both question Spike Lee's representations of women.[9] According to hooks, the cultural production of Black men is scrutinized more intensely than the cultural production of others for what is described as its sexism, particularly by white feminists. hooks seems not to understand why this should be the case, but, as with any oppositional political group, white feminists are looking for potential allies. The logic is that since African American men have suffered the oppression that comes from a racist society, they must have an understanding of how women suffer from a sexist society. However, it is not necessarily the case that the understanding of one form of oppression will entail the understanding of another. Furthermore, insofar as Black men participate in being constructed as men in our social order, it is not surprising that they would therefore collude in male privilege. A similar incredulity arises when Black feminists encounter racism among white feminists. Often they seem to be angrier at white feminists than at anyone else for their participation in white supremacy. Feminists should, according to this scheme, have a greater understanding of racist oppression, since they have an understanding of gender oppression. But insofar as someone is white, she also participates in the privileges of white supremacy. Finally, there is also the problem of "divide and conquer": domination works in part by pitting disempowered groups against each other (the famous "Black on Black violence" we heard about during apartheid in South Africa, or the stories about Blacks versus Jews in New York, or Koreans versus Blacks during the Los Angeles rebellion), and thus deflecting attention away from economic, political, and social policies that apportion scarce resources and set up competition among groups for those resources.

One of the dynamics that often underlie "racial" and "gender" antagonism is class resentment. Laura Kipnis, in an essay about middle-class feminist antagonism toward pornography, examines the male readership of *Hustler* in class terms in an attempt to clarify its particular virulence vis-à-vis women.[10] Her essay indicates some of the ways consciousness of one oppression may interact in contradictory fashion with other forms of oppression. She argues that *Hustler*'s "offensive" representations of women are an expression of class resentment, and that since middle-class femininity is the symbol *par excellence* of class privilege in mainstream culture, *Hustler* targets precisely this femininity as the object of its hostilities. She also argues that *Hustler* self-consciously pokes fun at middle-class "taste," thus reveling in what is improper, gross, disgusting, and tasteless, as an expression of the popular body's revolt against containment and discipline. However, *Hustler* magazine expresses its class antagonism or class resentment, and that of its readers, by attacking specifically upper-class women (*qua* women), thus bringing them "down" to the level of the working-class consciousness of the magazine. Here class antagonism gets expressed through an attack on the women of the upper class rather than the men; women become the primary "carriers" of class privilege.[11]

Thus misogyny, or sex domination, works to define the woman as the property of the upper-class man (if class antagonism is the focus) or the white man (if race domination is the focus). Once it is possible to view women as property, then it is possible to view the woman as the possession of the upper-class male whom the dominated wish to attack, hurt, defeat, or fight against in some other way. This particular masculine class antagonism works by "stealing" or "destroying" the (symbolic) property of the dominant masculine class. This is one of the reasons hooks insists that feminism is a necessary analytical and political tool in overcoming oppression and in the decolonization of colonized people. Without it, men battle over symbolic property and subsequently dehumanize women without in fact transforming the social structure that keeps the economy of domination in place.

Lee has been criticized for his representations of women, in part because he is viewed as a cultural hero, and so the pressures and the responsibilities—the accountability—are seen to be greater for him than for many other cultural workers. Lee, however, does not engage in this sort of mystified process of blaming the woman of the ruling class for class domination, or fighting back against domination across the body of the ruling-class woman. His analysis of class antagonism is, rather, quite progressive. Therefore, I would argue that if we critique his representations of women, we must also acknowledge the complexity of his vision compared with traditional representations of class conflict.

Various "battle of the sexes" arguments are set up in Lee's 1989 film *Do the Right Thing*: between Mother Sister and Da Mayor, between Tina and Mookie, and between Jade and Mookie. How do these battles coincide with what is being said about sexual politics in the film? The most glaring absence, if we are to critique Lee's analysis of gender and his treatment of women in the film, is an absence visible throughout mainstream filmic representations that introduce sexual politics into their texts: it is the absence of female bonding, or the solidarity that would suggest an autonomous realm of female subjectivity. The absence, in other words, of something that would suggest that women may have political agendas that do not directly relate to and through men.

I do not entirely agree with hooks when she says that in Lee's film, "gender and class are not evoked as forces which shape the construction of racial identity" ("Counter-Hegemonic Art," 177). *Do the Right Thing* (1989) is quite brilliant and specific in demonstrating how class antagonism works. Most often the oppressed class does not in fact "fight the power" itself, but instead attacks a contiguous group of people that is slightly above its rung on the class ladder. Lee analyzes how and why this occurs, thus implicitly (although not explicitly) providing an explanation for why class antagonism among men so often takes the form of an attack on women rather than on other men. Thus we see in this Brooklyn neighborhood that class resentment functions against the two slightly more empowered groups, the Koreans and the Italian Americans, who might be called petit bourgeois because they own property and profit directly from the "underclass" of the neighborhood. The three men who sit with their backs against the wall illustrate this phenomenon through the economic and political speculation they engage in about property-owning Korean grocers. What they do not mention, because it is not visible to them, is the way Korean immigrants to the United States have often entered into a network of family and community mutual economic assistance. Often these immigrants can obtain loans, for they enter with some connections already established and with a certain amount of capital, albeit modest, to invest. Cocoanut's observation that "it must be because we're Black" draws attention to how racial difference functions in relation to class: racism works specifically and differentially, particularly in conjunction with immigration. African Americans are often denied loans and thus prevented from accumulating enough capital to begin to set up a business like the pizzeria or the grocery store.

We can also see how this form of class resentment functioned in the Los Angeles rebellion, where the discourse of interracial conflict—at least as it was most widely represented—centered on Blacks and Korean Americans.[12] The naturalizing of racial antagonisms (as in "different folks just hate each other") works to obscure the very real social and material factors that determine this sort of conflict: the fact that the two groups are in contact with each other, whereas the ruling class is far removed; and the fact that class antagonisms arise from a very specific, differential economic relationship between each group and the dominant economy.[13] A group that is not analyzed but is mentioned in the riff of racist slurs in *Do the Right Thing* are Jews. The traditional inner-city conflict between Blacks and Jews is also informed by this kind of class resentment, where Jews are differentially racialized from African Americans: they are property owners but still marginalized, incompletely enfranchised in "white America."

Lee also illustrates class resentment's connection to racialization by making Pino, the most racist member of the Italian American family, also the character who most morphologically resembles African Americans. Mookie says to him, "your hair is kinkier than mine," and indeed it is precisely because Pino looks Black that he works harder than anyone else to distinguish himself in superiority, in status and class, from the African Americans of the neighborhood. It is his likeness that informs his excessive hatred. He complains that his friends at school liken him to the residents of Bedford Stuyvesant. He constructs himself as superior and different from the others through an excessive racialization: "I am not like them because I am white and white is better than black." He is, in other words, the one most threatened through his resemblance with, rather than his difference from, African Americans.

This brings me to an aspect of Lee's representation that has gone largely unremarked by critics, who themselves make the mistake of insufficiently examining racialization. When commenting on the film, the press often failed to distinguish between whiteness in general and the question of Italian Americans. But that specificity cannot be overlooked in Lee's vision. To do so demonstrates how it is just as problematic to create the culturally dominant as one monolithic group as it is to construct the "other" as a nameless, faceless, and nonspecific "oppressed" identity. Lee makes it clear that the specificity of the antagonism that emerges has to do with the differential racialization of so-called white groups as well; the antagonisms arise because the whites are Italian Americans, and thus only one rung above the Blacks on the class scale, and closely resembling African Americans in culture, customs, and morphology.[14] Casual prejudice, Lee seems to say, occurs among all sorts of ethnically differentiated groups (note how prejudiced everyone seems to be in this film), but it is the specifics of class, an economic relation, in combination with the particular way racism works in the United States that produces the explosive situation that results in tragedy.

hooks argues that few critics have seen this film as a serious indictment of contemporary Black liberation struggle, as she does; she also suggests that the film is unconscious of the way it testifies to the failure of that struggle (176). However, I think it can be argued that the film does reveal a certain "self-consciousness" in commenting about the failure of the sixties to provide a clear direction or program for the future of African American liberation struggles, whether or not we agree with its critique. When the film first appeared, one of the debates focused on which quotation at the end—Martin Luther King, Jr.'s or Malcolm X's—was the "right" or "recommended" one. The corollary question that arises, that is, the question in response to the film's imperative title, *Do the Right Thing*, is, what *is* the right thing to do? Which of the two recommendations is right? The one hooks and Wallace refer to as the "integrationist/assimilationist" argument, perhaps inaccurately named, but most often associated with Martin Luther King, Jr., or the "nationalist/separatist" argument, again perhaps inaccurately named, but associated with Malcolm X? Anti-violence or violence in self-defense?[15] How, in other words, is the recommendation to "fight the power" to be carried out? The subtlety of Lee's film makes this difficult to determine.

I do not think there is a single message to derive from *Do the Right Thing*. What makes Lee such an interesting director and cultural producer is that he is willing to represent ambiguity, and he is also willing to allow his team (the actors in particular) to shape the narrative in some of their own ways. For example, in this film he chose two prominent Italian American actors to play the roles of Sal (Danny Aiello) and Vito (John Turturro), and allowed them to shape their roles in ways that avoided the gross stereotyping of Italians.[16] He also gave the role of the most supermilitant neonationalist Black character in the movie, Buggin' Out, to a Black Italian, Giancarlo Esposito, thus rendering ironic, from an extra-diagetic point of view, the interracial conflict depicted in the movie.

Another issue that arises in connection with the film's messages— an issue that arises frequently with regard to films understood to be conveying a political message—is framed in terms of "necessity." Is it "necessary," in other words, to depict a particular act or event in order to get one's message across? A corollary to this question is the question of advisability. If someone is trying to convey a particular message, is it advisable to do it in one way rather than another? Concerning Lee's film, I have often heard white students ask whether showing the police killing Radio Raheem was "necessary." It is worth asking ourselves why we use the category of necessity to talk about this kind of representation. Such a question ties the cultural worker to a tradition of liberal political debate that may not, in fact, be perceived as effective. The question may also, it is worth noting, belong to a tradition of political engagement that is different from the one adopted by the oppositional politics of a given group. Mainstream debates about representations construed as political also raise questions about justifiability (is the way a phenomenon is represented justifiable or not, and on what grounds?); value (the question of whether a representation has any "socially redeeming value," and the relation of redemption to culture); accuracy, truth, and distortion. Why such categories are invoked may be explained in part by the way the word "representation," in the context of oppositional or politically engaged art, has at least a double meaning: a depiction (as in a visual representation of something) and political representation. Thus, perhaps, we bring criteria for the second kind of representation to bear on the first, asking of a given representation how representative it is.

Representation, however, does not function in this manner. It is true that a representation of the world, or some aspect of it, is a construction of that world, a creation that may try to pass itself off as the real world. But the effect of "passing itself off as" is called ideology—a certain way of presenting the world that declares itself to be the truth of the world, that seems so self-evident that we take it as the truth. There is no way to "avoid" ideological representation; there are, rather, ways of analyzing what a particular ideology is and how it constructs the "truth" it wants us to believe. In the case of a fictional text, such as Lee's *Do the Right Thing*, we know that to a certain extent it is not simply a picture of the world as it is, though it may be an argument about how Lee envisions the world. It is something we call fiction, and thus it declares itself deliberately as an eccentric creation: perhaps true, perhaps not.

Finally, some would argue that it was "necessary" to show the police killing Radio Raheem because not enough white folks know that police kill Black men; that is why the crowd is chanting "Howard Beach," and why the film credits indicate that the film is dedicated to the memory of several African Americans who were killed by police and by other acts of racist violence. In this respect, the film acts as a kind of testimonial: a call to remember what has been done, lest we forget. It performs a consciousness-raising exercise. *Do the Right Thing* thus has a political mission: it explicitly ties itself to the world outside its representation. It is a narrative of resistance that announces its political engagement and calls for its audience to take the historical context into account and to act: "Vote!" is Señor Love Daddy's radio announcement at the end of the film, the only unambiguous message of the movie.

C. Rap, Rock, Resistance

Popular music has become a particularly contested arena in which questions of race and gender are debated, and rap has come to signify the popular resistance of Black youth in the United States. I want to consider rap music as a form of resistance. Barbara Harlow argues that poetry is the genre par excellence of resistance literature. Poetry may act as a kind of cultural manifesto of a given movement. Rap too is a form of poetry: it is recitative, it rhymes, and it has a distinct meter and rhythm. In many ways, we might regard the rap explosion as a kind of manifesto of what hooks calls the new neonationalism among African Americans, Chicanos, and occasionally other groups in the United States today ("Counter-Hegemonic Art").

As hooks argues, and as the documentary *Rap City Rhapsody* (1990) demonstrates, the rapid commodification of rap in the music industry and on MTV means that the genre does not remain "purely" an expression of the people, and sometimes what is conveyed are more the effects of resistance than resistance itself. But rap has also been responsible for bringing to light issues of racism, police violence, drug use, and sexism and putting them out there for public debate in a way that many politicians and policy makers have not been successful at doing. Ice-T's song "Cop Killer," for example, has helped to raise public consciousness about the problem of police violence in our country, while the boycotts of this song have increased public debate about the role of police in "keeping the peace," and the implication of police justice in white supremacist or racist modes of domination in the United States.

2 Live Crew created a stir in the public arena for the purported obscenity and sexism of their album *As Nasty as They Wanna Be*. The attack on their lyrics triggered a public discussion about sexuality in relation to race. It also provoked conversations about the social context of rap: where it comes from, what it stands for, and what its purpose is. Again, just to highlight one of the effects of popular culture, what is really noticeable in the various controversies around rap is the degree to which "representation" is taken as a reflection of the real, or as a kind of advocacy. Ice-T was seen as advocating violence against the police, no matter how much he argued that the character in his song was a persona, and 2 Live Crew was seen as advocating violence against women. This underscored the extent to which cultural production is understood to be political, understood to have influence, and understood to have social consequences as well.[17]

In his analysis of rock, Simon Frith cautions us not to assume that popular music is a direct expression of the street. Rather, we should understand it as a conscious artistic choice on the part of writers, producers, singers, and performers:

> This is not to say rock isn't oppositional to mainstream adult/bourgeois values, but rather, that such ideological sounds are a matter of conscious decision, not immediate street expression. Musicians whose own social and educational backgrounds can be varied thus come together in their use of an oppositional voice, but the commitment is as much aesthetic as political. ("The Cultural Study of Popular Music," 176)

He continues, "music is not just something young people like and do. It is in many respects the model for their involvement in culture" (177). He thus suggests that we look at popular music as a particular model of a certain relation to culture that foregrounds opposition as an aesthetic value. This is, in fact, something hooks complains about in relation to Spike Lee, for she argues that when Black nationalism is aestheticized, as it has been, it loses its political oppositional force and becomes one more commodity to be consumed ("Counter-Hegemonic Art," 177–78).

Frith's essay is a critique of the way some cultural studies intellectuals look at popular music as a pure expression of resistance. He argues that intellectuals are partly responsible for the myth of popular music as the expression of rootless, homeless, rebellious resistance, a kind of postmodern resistance that everyone can consume or participate in because it is diffused throughout the culture. Further, Frith argues that this approach has, in turn, had an influence on popular music. Indeed, we might argue that the category of world music is, in part, a result of a deliberate construction of an effect of resistance through the use of Third World musicians and singers.[18] Frith also comments on the role of African American music and culture in American pop and rock by saying that what is African comes to stand in for "the shocking, exotic, primitive other of bourgeois respectability," and for "nature opposed to culture"; the myth of the natural is thus imposed on African and Afro-Caribbean music (180).[19]

Frith also points out that women are often excluded from the domain of rock. But rather than focus on its exclusionary nature, he contends, one should regard rock as a homosocial space. In his view, rock culture, particularly in Britain, comes to stand for how boys can have fun together (without girls) and how desire between men can be expressed across class lines.[20] The issue of women's voices in rap has changed considerably in recent years. Many African American women are commenting—from within rap itself—on their exclusion from the arena of rap cultural production. Queen Latifah's "Ladies First," a song about the preeminence of women in various arenas of the social, comes to mind, as well as the prodigious output of groups such as Salt-N-Pepa. I do not think we have heard much yet from gay pop and rock musicians who reclaim the space of pop and/or rock as a homo-erotic space, although there were significant numbers of groups that did so in the seventies, such as the Village People with their hit song "YMCA."

D. Sound and Story

As I mentioned, one reason one would want to ask questions about the relation between popular music and political resistance or subversion is that popular music has become a domain of political discussion in public culture. Furthermore, right-wing attempts at censorship in the United States also bring popular music or youth music into the forefront of questions of resistance and opposition, in spite of the fact that censorship may be, at times, yet another marketing strategy on the part of producers and distributors, since they know that the production of scandalous news about scandalous content can incite buyers to consume the object of the scandal.

A genre of music that has acquired phenomenal recent popularity is the soundtrack album. It used to be that soundtrack albums either addressed the genre of musical (where the soundtrack, as in opera, was "the film" in some significant ways) or accompanied concert films or films about rock groups. In recent years, the soundtrack album has become a genre unto itself, regardless of the quality, popularity, or genre of the film, and sometimes with little or no relation to the narrative of the film, although there is often a thematic continuity: films about Black drug dealers or Black life in the urban United States feature rap music and hip hop, for example.

The soundtracks I want to examine are associated with the films *The Bodyguard* (Mick Jackson, 1992), *Waiting to Exhale* (Forest Whitaker, 1995), and *Dead Man Walking* (Tim Robbins, 1995). Each highlights a certain dimension of the political in relation to the popular: two of them specifically feature African American women (as actors and as popular musicians), and *Dead Man Walking* addresses a widespread political debate in the United States about the death penalty.

When one raises the question of pop music in relation to the political (and these albums, although hybrid in musical genre, fall primarily within the category of pop), I think one has to mention that pop—at least in the United States—already occupies a degraded political position in relation to certain other genres: folk, for example, which is the people's music, and rock, which, in the sixties, came to stand in for the countercultural revolution. Pop is even degraded vis-à-vis hip hop, which is also seen to be politically resistive in that it emanates from urban Black life and protest. Pop is also regarded as a degraded musical form: typically, it does not feature "artist" musicians; the music is not considered original or creative; it privileges the vocal over the musical; and the vocalist is usually not thought to be the artist either, but is rather thought to be ventriloquizing. In addition, the vocalist is, more often than not, female.[21] Thus pop is the domain of the feminine—the not-art, the not-serious, the not–politically resistive. It is no wonder, in fact, that pop is the domain of the feminine; as a degraded genre—like science fiction, mystery, and the humanities in academe—it is an arena of female class aspirancy. It is also potentially a space where women can achieve some agency in the domain of representation, since rock is still, by and large, masculine and white, while hip hop is still predominantly masculine and Black. While pop seems to represent the abdication of political resistance through musical/lyric forms in the social, it may nevertheless turn out to afford some space for the articulation of less hegemonically represented and representable subjectivities and agencies.

As I have argued, in current mass media and pop culture in the United States, the progressive dimensions of what is called multiculturalism, such as the specific "complaints" of African Americans and white women (these complaints being understood in very liberal individualist terms), are being recognized, and it is interesting to examine simultaneously how these are also appropriated for other, usually conservative, sometimes reactionary, political purposes. The films I examine here and their soundtracks illustrate some of the contradictory political energies of popular cultural productions. Specifically I want to ask, what are the possibilities of music and song retaining a certain oppositional or progressive force—a legacy, perhaps, of the sixties—in relation to the more conservative accompanying visual narratives for these songs?

The Bodyguard, a movie whose message is unrelentingly reactionary in its embrace of a certain understanding of multiculturalism, features a white man, Kevin Costner (*the* white man perhaps, given his career as white liberal actor in films such as *Dances with Wolves*), as a former secret serviceman (presidential bodyguard) who goes to work as the bodyguard for Rachel Marron ("brown" Rachel), played by the pop singer and actress Whitney Houston, who is the proverbial single Black mother of a son. Here we have a situation that recognizes Hollywood's history of African Americans in "helping roles" in film and progressively changes that situation by presenting two stars, one white, one Black, whose fame is at least equal. The film confers agency on the woman, makes her ambitious, successful, and aggressive; nevertheless, it also uses its narrative line to chastise her for this agency via the threats to her life and the sacrifice of the hero (he puts himself in harm's way to save her).

The story scripts some very conservative politics around race: the great and good white man "saves" the Black woman and her child, in the name of service to the nation (which is, I think, the point of his being a presidential bodyguard), while she teaches him to have a heart. Her true enemy, the film concludes, the one who is trying to kill her, is her sister, the woman with whom Houston sings a gospel duet ("Jesus Loves Me") presented in a different version (i.e., not as a female duet) on the soundtrack album.

By contrast, the soundtrack is co-executively produced by Whitney Houston and features the Dolly Parton song "I Will Always Love You," which became a major hit in the United States.[22] In spite of the film's reactionary messages, its musical dimension features a major African American pop vocalist—the most popular pop vocalist perhaps, besides Aretha Franklin, to consistently bring the gospel tradition into the forefront of her musical production. Indeed, the first time this song appears in the film, it is sung by a male country and western vocalist, and Houston remarks, "This is a kind of cowboy song"; thus the reemergence of the song (eliding its female source) as a Houston hit proposes the triumph of Black pop/gospel over white country and western, and creates a tacit "battle of the races" through song. Music thus reverses the traditionally paternalist thematics of the film's gender narrative, for Houston is clearly the active talent and the orchestrating force of the musical production (on the album cover she is the single foregrounded image, while Costner is portrayed in multiple, little images in the background). Indeed, the movie could also be seen to be about launching Houston's career as an actress; about foregrounding MTV as the preferred visual genre; and about bringing into focus the relation between politics and superstardom ("Politics and show biz, it's the same thing these days" is a line from the film). The politically and economically progressive dimension here remains within a liberal individualist framework, for it operates on the level of individual agency, the agency of a Black woman who is marked and identified as African American in terms of cultural tradition (gospel).

Waiting to Exhale is another text in which one might read a political gap between the soundtrack and the film.[23] The movie, based on the 1992 novel by Terry McMillan, features a group of extremely bourgeois Black women looking for love in all the wrong places, so relentlessly pursuing heterosexuality that one cannot help but think of the lesbian alternative. *Waiting to Exhale* prominently features Black women and seems, on the surface, to be feminist in that it presents a liberal interpretation of the heterosexual feminist complaint that "all men are dogs." Of course, because she conforms more closely to traditional expectations of proper and "docile" femininity, the woman who gets the good man is older, less wealthy, by all the social markers less ambitious and successful in her aspirations, and the single mother of a son. Although the movie ends in a moment of female bonding, its narrative drive will not permit the possibility of an autonomously female, or even nonheterosexual, solution to the women's problem.

The soundtrack, on the other hand, celebrates Black women, Black women together and Black women alone, but Black women exclusively. Furthermore, the one song that describes a married woman's desertion by her husband lyrically foregrounds a more **materialist**— and thus, I would argue, a more authentic—female/feminist complaint than the wealth-saturated rage-fest we are treated to when Angela Bassett's millionaire husband abandons her and his millions:

> *Not Gon' Cry*
> . . . Eleven years, out of my life
> Besides the kids I've got nothing to show
> Wasted my years, a fool of a wife
> I shoulda left your ass long time ago
> . . . I was your lover and your secretary
> Working every day of the week
> Was at the job when no one else was there
> Helping you get on your feet
> Eleven years of sacrifice
> And you can leave me at the drop of a dime.[24]

In the film, this lyrical description does not apply: three of the women benefit from comfortably funded leisure time, and the divorcee receives a house worth about half a million dollars, a country house in Acapulco, a Mercedes Benz station wagon, and a $1.2 million share of her husband's company.

Furthermore, "race" is foregrounded in the movie as the problem of Black men dating white women: the wealthy husband deserts his wife in order to be with a white woman. Here again, however, the lesson is liberal: if it is love, and if he stays with her till death, then we have to learn to look past color (as long as she dies, and as long as he dedicates his life to working for civil rights, as is the case with the character of the lawyer played by Wesley Snipes in the film).

Waiting to Exhale thus liberalizes, and also trivializes, the material stakes of a certain feminist complaint and relentlessly heterosexualizes female bonding, while tacitly setting up an all-Black female **genealogy** for a musical/vocal tradition that combines blues, gospel, and pop. It seems all the more ironic, then, that there is such an insistence on heterosexuality in the narrative, including what seems to be an insistence that female blues addresses the domain of heterosexual conflict, when, on the contrary, it is known that the blues was also a "queer" space.

Indeed, part of the work of denial that this film performs is to represent homosexuality and then distance it from the women, for the two gay characters represented are men. The soundtrack, on the contrary, foregrounds the female genealogy, the blend of musical traditions, and the material dimensions of the feminist complaint. In addition, the visual presentation of the soundtrack album features the group of women on its cover, as well as on its inside front and back covers, affirming "girls together," without simultaneously insisting on the heterocentrism of that space.

Although it does not feature the question of racialization—the most obvious way mainstream and popular culture understands the problem of multiculturalism in the United States—I would like to discuss *Dead Man Walking* because it is one of the most egregious examples of an appropriation of liberal or progressive political impulses for conservative ends, and because it reinterprets "multiculturalism" so that the term is not a liberal domestic racial reference but a gesture in the direction of "internationalism": world music, or, as the director, Tim Robbins, writes, "music of the world." "Music of the world" provides, for the director, the "spiritual" dimension of the film that could not be addressed by "hymns, organs, gospel."[25]

Why is it not possible for gospel music and Cajun/Delta blues to speak to the spiritual dimension of the film? Robbins says that they are too regional and that the story is universal, so the answer "lay in a meeting ground between, a mix of the south and the music of the world." He appropriates international "multiculturalism" precisely in order to avoid the highly "regional" or local political issues at stake, which are, nevertheless, symptomatically figured by "the South," where the story takes place. Those local political issues have to do with the use of the death penalty in the United States; the highly specific ways the death penalty is discussed; and the disavowed knowledge, a disavowal confirmed by the U.S. Supreme Court, that the majority of death row inmates are Black men, that Black men are disproportionately given the death penalty in the United States, and that this fact is an indicator of racism. For the soundtrack, Robbins chooses the Pakistani singer Nusrat Fateh Ali Khan and an Armenian dudouk player, Djivan Gasparyan. The rest of the singers are white men and women from folk, rock, and country and western, genres more traditionally associated with political protest, but also more specifically white.

In the guise of a liberal protest against the inhumaneness of the death penalty, the narrative of *Dead Man Walking* ultimately confirms and consecrates the logic of the death penalty, and consecrates it with Catholicism (although the Catholic Church officially opposes the death penalty), thus symptomatically avoiding a reference to Christian Protestant fundamentalism. "Make your peace with God for the wrong you did and die forgiven, but die. Accept your fate," the film seems to counsel. There is no mass political protest against the death penalty. Instead, we see the murdered couple appear as "ghost" over-lays at the scene of death, to witness their vindication; in spite of how "wrong" the penalty is said to be in the course of the movie, the film operates according to the logic of an equalizing vindication. Here we have a perhaps unwitting appropriation of a liberal, indeed a theological, argument against the state's right to inflict the punishment of death for wrongs done, toward the end of justifying a logic of retribution that is then sanctified by the church. It is also massively symptomatic that the inmate is white; translate the color and the message becomes frighteningly ominous.

The music, on the other hand, argues against the death penalty and uses salt-of-the-earth musicians to do it. It also refers cynically to religion's hypocritical role in justifying actions such as the death penalty, in stark opposition to its own explicit dictates. The devastating effect of the songs contrasts radically with the narrative of the film; the songs are uncompromising in their refusal of the death penalty as a means of punishment and render complex many of the issues that are flattened out in the film.

Can anything be salvaged from this? Is there a way that the current success of pop as a mass media genre (a success greater than the success of films in that it is more profitable for marketers) can be strategically appropriated to run interference on the conservative containment or reactionary appropriation of liberal "multicultural" values and political aims? Can musicians, singers, performers, some of whom take on the resistive, oppositional, even subversive legacies of their musical traditions and genealogies, insert some kind of resistive agency into the relentlessly appropriative narratives of such popular visual culture? What good can it do, if any? This exploration of the gap between resistive musical traditions and liberal or conservative cultural fantasies demonstrates some of the complexities within the category of the popular that make of it an ideologically contradictory domain.

| S I X |

Technocultures

A. Technocultures and Postmodernism

In this chapter I would like to explore cultural productions that ambivalently represent postindustrial society's romance and disillusionment with advanced technological developments. The representations examined here present technoculture as an important dimension of both the present and the future, and construct a variety of responses, both utopian and dystopian, to that culture. Technology is the defining mark of late-twentieth-century First World existence in the popular imagination, and thus it is a particularly fruitful terrain for social and political analysis.

The texts I am discussing, in their disillusionment with the promises of industrial society and better living through advanced technology, engage in some form or another with the question of the postmodern. Postmodernism suffers from a surfeit of definition, and my ~an excess~ characterization here simplifies the range of meanings the concept encompasses. For the purposes of this survey of technocultural fantasies, the postmodern can be thought of as a historical designator, referring temporally to the period following World War II in Northwestern Europe and the United States. In the wake of the Holocaust, **Enlightenment** notions of the power of rationality to achieve social good are seen to have failed utterly; this includes the realization that not only can reason not save us from self-destruction and evil, but that reason itself can be harnessed in the service of diabolical goals. Added to this sense of the failure of reason and the triumph of destructive irrationality are fears of a nuclear apocalypse, so that the threat of imminent self-destruction becomes part of the failure of Enlightenment ideals to save the world.

The postmodern also refers to the postindustrial, the turn away from industrial optimism and visions of infinite prosperity through production, to the industrial decay of late capitalist urban centers. The confrontation with ecological disaster also contributes to the atmosphere of postmodernism. "Next to high-tech, its waste," writes Giuliana Bruno of the postmodern Los Angeles city landscape represented in Ridley Scott's *Blade Runner* (1982).[1] Postmodernism also refers to an aesthetic, one that has to do in part with reactions to this deeply pessimistic, nearly apocalyptic and dystopian vision of the postindustrial world.

MTV is often cited as an illustration of postmodernist aesthetics: fragmented images (pastiche) and a sense of disjuncture in time and space (time is no longer linear, it jumps around between past, present, and future, it speeds up, slows down).[2] The present does not follow the past; rather, everything is on one flat simultaneous plane, and past, present, and future all appear in the present as a collection of images. There is no sense of history as that which came before; instead, history is treated as a set of images, a collection of representations without context. Thus, for example, Frederic Jameson and others use "schizophrenia" to characterize postmodern consciousness.[3] Bruno adds, "The industrial machine was one of production, the postindustrial machine, one of reproduction. A major shift occurs: the alienation of the subject is replaced by the fragmentation of the subject, its dispersal in representation" (69).

The postmodern aesthetic involves the dominance of the notion of representation. The visual predominates in a society of the spectacle.[4] The postmodern dismantles the notion of a real behind the copy; it is the age of the copy, or what is called the **simulacrum**, a copy that has no real as its referent, no real as that from which it originated. It is simulation. Scott's film *Blade Runner* features the Replicants, the better-than-people copies of people who never existed, copies that do not originate in the real but are pure and perfect reproductions, without a past, without a history, without a future, existing in a schizophrenic present (Bruno, 68).[5]

*MTV AESTHETIC **

Another way to think about postmodernism, which I simplify here, is as the projection of symptomatic anxieties on the part of Western intellectuals. These are anxieties about the waning role of the postindustrial West in the future narrative of the earth, especially if the role was once conceived as that of the bearer of civilization, improvement, and progress. Postmodernism reflects the sense that what the West contributes to the future is destruction and decay, and that history, as a process of positive transformation, will no longer be in Western hands.[6] The response to such disillusionment with the promises of postindustrial culture is a kind of despair, a withdrawal into the self-contemplation of self-destruction. This is the dystopic aspect of postmodern cultural production. The replacement of history and narrative with representation, fragments of images all in the present; the reveling in the accumulation of commodities and representations without trying to connect them to stories of production or histories of how they got there may be thought of as aspects of the denial involved in the West's postmodern consciousness.

However, in this postmodern aesthetic of denial or despair there hovers the trace of "real" history and the reluctant acknowledgment that a future that may have nothing to do with us exists out there, accompanied by a powerful nostalgia for the way things used to be. In William Gibson's novel *Neuromancer*, as we shall see, this takes the form of the occasional nostalgia for nature that is linked to woman, to sexual difference, and to desire.[7] In *Blade Runner* history is all-important, for history is what ultimately distinguishes human from replicant.

In *Neuromancer* the recognition of the future as taking place "elsewhere" is figured by the release of the AI (Artificial Intelligence). The AI returns to the protagonist, Case, at the end of the novel to say, "I'm not Wintermute now. I'm the matrix" (269); it has merged with and talks to other AIs in the net. In *Neuromancer*, then, the future, even the future of the virtual no-place that is **cyberspace**, does not lie in the hands of "meat" (the term used to refer to human beings) at all, but in the minds of artificial intelligences, that is, in personality, and in mind without body. *Blade Runner*, on the other hand, seems to question the very notion of what constitutes the human and suggests, through the romance between the protagonist (a human) and the beautiful replicant Rachel, that the future may involve a hybridization of the biological and the technological. In this respect, *Blade Runner* shares the more optimistic vision of the future described by Butler's trilogy; humans have indeed exhausted their time, but that does not mean that humanity will disappear. Instead, what is understood to constitute humanity will change, adapt, and transform itself. These narratives might be said to be posthumanist in their visions of the future and, as posthumanist, they find a way beyond the impasses of postmodern despair and denial.

One of the predominant themes in this discussion of technocultures will be the relationship between technoculture and feminist thinking. Technology has been and is viewed as a predominantly masculine domain, indeed, as defining late-twentieth-century advanced capitalist Western masculinity. Yet much of the commentary about technology and its social consequences is coming from feminist camps, and many popular cultural representations of technoculture involve some attempt to talk about women and technology, or women and science. This can be in part attributed to two factors. First, as Zoë Sofia argues in her essay "Exterminating Fetuses," technoculture constructs itself in relation to the world according to the dichotomy "culture-man/nature-woman."[8] The second factor is that some of the most consistent critiques of technoculture and organized protests against it have come from women's movements. The antinuclear and peace movements have been articulated in feminist terms, and ecological movements have privileged a feminine, if not feminist, relationship to the world: love your mother. Accepting, in part, the dichotomies set up by technoculture—perhaps for strategic purposes—women's movements have promoted what is viewed as a distinctly "female" relationship to life, involving nurturance; respect for life; caring; symbiosis rather than conquest; peace rather than war; emotional warmth rather than cold rationality; heart over mind. A whole series of values associated with the feminine and the maternal are enlisted to argue for the preservation of the earth. The degree to which some of the discourse of ecological responsibility relies on stereotypical notions of the relation between woman and nature suggests, even more strongly, how "woman" becomes inevitably entangled with discourses of technology in our culture.

Sofia outlines the influential paradigm of technoculture that is set up in Stanley Kubrick's 1968 science fiction film *2001: A Space Odyssey*. She understands current popular fantasies about technology in representation as masculine appropriations of (women's) biological capacity to reproduce, and connects these to the myth of Zeus devouring the Titan Methis. Methis is pregnant at the time; Zeus, after devouring her, gives birth to Athena, the goddess of wisdom and technology, through his head (she is his brainchild). The myth thus enacts a displacement, in the domain of reproduction, from the female uterus to the male belly to the paternal brain ("Exterminating Fetuses," 51); technological birthing then replaces biological birthing. Sofia invokes the "sexo-semiotics" of technology to describe a representational system where all technology is reproductive technology. Technology, she argues, is about reproduction. As such, and as the product of a specifically masculine technology of reproduction, technoculture also carries within it a certain ambivalence: an awareness of its appropriative gesture and a fear that nature will seek revenge (48–49).

B. William Gibson's *Neuromancer*

It is impossible to overestimate the importance of William Gibson's *Neuromancer*, both for the history of imaginings of cyberspace and VR (virtual reality) research, and for the SF genre of cyberpunk. As both Allucquere Stone and Peter Fitting note, Gibson's work represents crossover science fiction, that is, work that circulates outside the traditional science fiction readership and introduces a much larger constituency of readers to the genre.[9] Stone argues that Gibson's importance for "epoch four" of virtual communities, the one she calls virtual space and cyberpunk, is that he crystallized a new community through the publication of his book. *Neuromancer* constructs or creates a subculture, including a slang appropriate to that subculture, a style, a stance, a mode of relating to and rebelling against the dominant culture. How does *Neuromancer* work to set up recognition codes for its constituency? How would we go about describing the subculture that it creates?

In "The Lessons of Cyberpunk," Fitting argues that cyberpunk's defiance lies in its reaction against science fiction's increasing commercial success and the repetitive reliance on profitable formulas. But he also points out that "the very rejection of the mainstream has been converted into a merchandising label that suggests a trendy, on-the-edge lifestyle." "It is not punk," he says, "but an image of punk, a fashion emptied of any oppositional content that has become a signifier to be used in a countertrend marketing strategy. The outlaw stance of some of cyberpunk's early champions corresponds primarily to images of rebellion as mediated by MTV" (297). This characterization points to an important cautionary perspective for students of cultural studies: rebellion and defiance do not necessarily signal subversion or revolution. Resistance is not necessarily progressive in its oppositional stance. I want to use Gibson's *Neuromancer* as a way of meditating on the problematic politics of "resistive" subcultural communities as they are imagined by technoculture.

Stone raises the question of community in relation to electronic communication and makes the observation that

> Many of the engineers currently debating the form and nature of cyberspace are the young turks of computer engineering, men in their late teens and twenties, and they are preoccupied with the things with which postpubescent men have always been preoccupied. This rather steamy group will generate the codes and descriptors by which bodies in cyberspace are represented. (103–4)

The developers of cyberspace and the cyberpunk readership may be said to constitute a kind of "cyberfraternity," a fraternity of adolescent and postadolescent boys in virtual space. Such communities might be said to resemble, in some ways, the more familiar community of the college campus fraternity. The convergences between the two communities suggest a rethinking of the masculine vision of the cyberworld as represented by *Neuromancer*. What are the implications for our socially lived future in virtual communities, given what Stone says about the ways real-life young men in the industry are envisioning and fashioning the social world of cyberspace and the bodily world of the agents and surrogates of "the meat"?

One might want to think about this in the psychoanalytic terms of **oedipal** rebellion, the rebellion of sons against their fathers. Fraternities, in a certain way, represent the defiance of sons against the authority of fathers. Paternal authority is represented by the institution of the school, the university, the rules and regulations of sober, severe, paternal, and responsible conduct dictated to the university community. Campus fraternities rebel against these by consciously or semiconsciously enacting a "bad boy, I-don't-wanna-grow-up-and-be-responsible" answer to the responsibilities of patriarchal culture that they will have to assume in their turn. Paternal authority and paternal calls to duty are oppressive; they are, in fact, the law. Thus fraternities celebrate fraternal bonding rather than patriarchal bonding; they celebrate communities of male peers rather than communities defined by the patriarchal household. They also celebrate a defiance of the law, through illegal or excessive intoxication, rowdiness, and other forms of socially proscribed behavior. So far, this is what Andrew Ross calls the "protopolitical" potential of any subcultural formation, that is, a subculture's potential to resist the dominant social order and its imposed ideology.[10]

However, in fraternities this resistive energy does not, it seems, get translated into a progressive political program, a community that organizes itself to transform the social order by harnessing those resistive energies and channeling them into analyses and visions of social change. Psychoanalytically and politically described, we might say that fraternities serve a containment function for the potentially oppositional energies of adolescent males. Boys are permitted (by the patriarchy) to rebel (and this is why institutions often seem quite hypocritical in their simultaneous opposition to and sanction or approval of fraternity conduct), on the condition that after their four years of "letting off steam," they will accept their symbolic castration (which means their obedience to paternal dictates and laws) and grow up to assume those responsible patriarchal functions that, in fact, paternal law is preparing them for. In other words, they grow up to become and replace the patriarchs, the very same patriarchs they were rebelling against in college; thus their oppositional energy has been contained. One of the ways the patriarchy guarantees its reproduction and replacement, even from within the resistive and oppositional moment of fraternal bonding, is through a certain relation to women, the female body, and femininity.

The exercise of privilege over women, in the form of sexual violence, degradation, parody, and selective exclusion, guarantees an important mediation between and among the men, a mediation that will keep them from turning toward and loving each other, a mediation that will prevent homoeroticism and produce homosociality instead. Homosociality guarantees the control of social space by men only, while it also ensures that the fiction of a competitive structure (men competing for women) will persist and eventually take over once the men themselves become patriarchs.[11]

Hierarchy among men is necessary because without it, the fable goes, we would have anarchy; or, to put it differently, without hierarchy, patriarchy would not have a leg to stand on, because patriarchy depends on respect for paternal law, leaders, and commanders. This is one of the important and explicit reasons that the military persists in its proscription of homosexuals. According to the military, to permit homosexuality would undermine the chain of command, because the bonds of love between and among men would disregard the hierarchical arrangement, the "necessity" for some men to learn to command and others to learn to obey, even when obedience goes against any reasonable calculation of self-interest or survival (in other words, even when one knows that to obey means to be killed). The bonds of love between and among men would also mean that men would reject the philosophy of dying for the patriarchy (for the nation-state, the law of the land, the fathers who started the wars that the sons always have to fight and die for).

Another reason the abuse and/or degradation of women is necessary to the subcultural construction of fraternities is one that brings me back to the topic of technocultural science fiction. Stone writes,

> In psychoanalytic terms, for the young male, unlimited power first suggests the mother. The experience of unlimited power is both gendered, and, for the male, fraught with the need for control, producing an unre-

solvable need for reconciliation with an always absent structure of personality. An absent structure of personality is also another way of describing the peculiarly seductive character of the computer . . . as a second self. Both also constitute a constellation of responses to the simulation that deeply engage fear, desire, pleasure, and the need for domination, subjugation, and control. (108)

The technocultural world that cyberpunk and other recent science fiction narratives represent engages with the feminine in a peculiar way. There is the oedipalized relation to the mother as the first all-powerful female figure who dominates the infant boy (some examples include the computer in *Alien* [MU TH UR], the maternal drama in *Aliens*, and the matrix in *Neuromancer*). In the oedipal narrative, the mother is the boy's object of desire, an object of desire he is prevented from merging with by the law of the father, or by paternal interdiction. In the homosocial fraternal space of the fraternity, the delay between adolescence and adulthood involves a drama of the feminine; the mother haunts the space of fraternal bonding as the forbidden object of desire and also as the powerful force that once controlled the life of the boy. She is simultaneously desired and feared, feared not only because the father promises to punish the son for desiring the mother, but also because the mother once controlled the son. In the space of the fraternity, the forbidden figure of the mother is feminine difference, the feminine, women.

The feminine is constituted as a threat and an object of desire in the space of fraternal bonding; fraternal bonding in turn "eliminates" the woman as principle of division, by creating all-male peer bonding where the woman is the object (of conversation that goes on among men). On the other hand, because of the mother's perceived power over the son, she serves as the object of displacement for the patriarchal or paternal function; once again we have a situation where women, rather than fathers, patriarchy, or the state, are blamed for the young man's feelings of oppression. The mother, or the feminine, is blamed because she is what is different: there is not the same degree of identification with the mother as with the father. Further, to blame the father is dangerous because one might be harmed ("castrated," in psychoanalytic terms, but more literally harmed if we think

of the paternal as the state). To blame the father is also to refuse to
be a man, according to the terms in which masculinity is constructed
in our social order. The woman thus fulfills the function of scapegoat
in the homosocial culture of the fraternity (and, one might argue, in
the homosocial culture of patriarchy itself).

Does *Neuromancer* adopt this mythology of masculinity or does it
subvert it? One might argue that this question is important to answer
if, as Stone claims, it is primarily young men who are configuring the
social space of VR and the bodies of the future communities of cyberspace (103–4). If, as she argues, "Cyberspace can be viewed as a tool
kit for refiguring consciousness in order to permit things to go on in
much the same way" (110); and if cyberspace and virtual communities
are "flexible, lively, and practical adaptations to the real circumstances
that confront persons seeking community—part of the range of innov-
ative solutions to the drive for sociality . . . complex and ingenious
strategies for survival" (110–11), then it seems that it would be important to determine whether the virtual communities that will structure the future will indeed be a projection and/or realization of adolescent masculine visions of fraternal community. Will this be a community that enacts its ambivalence about the feminine and, in practice,
tends on the one hand to idealize the feminine (Ripley from the *Alien*
films) and, on the other, to demonize her (the alien, the computer)?
In either case, will the cyberspace community of the future include
feminine or female subjectivity at all? Will there be room for sexualities
and beings that do not adhere to Freudian family romances? Will there
be room for revolutionary ways of interacting socially and bodily not
only between men and women but also among men and among
women?

Gibson's depiction of the relationship between Case, the protagonist, and Molly, the "razor girl," does offer hope for a progressive
vision of the relationship between the sexes. Molly's femininity, like
that of Ripley in the *Alien* films, is unusual. She is a killer, and she
is stronger than Case; her body is described as machine-like, perfect
in its musculature and functionality. She is tough and heroic, like
Ripley. At a certain point in the novel, Case is forced to "inhabit"
her through the simstim (simulated stimulation). He takes on the

feeling of her physical being and her consciousness, but there inside her, he is powerless to control either her thoughts, her body, or her actions.

This might be an illustration of what Stone means when she says, "To become the **cyborg**, to put on the seductive and dangerous cybernetic space like a garment, is to put on the female" (109), and it also suggests the feminization of the male in relation to technocultures, that is, the observation that the new technocultural man is feminized by his relation to the prosthetic device. In *Neuromancer* this feminization is positively, not negatively, valorized. Thus we have what seems to be a progressive reimagining of the feminine in this world; masculine and feminine are brought into closer contact.[12] However, might we not also ask whether these female characters bear any relation to "women" at all, or do they enact precisely a masculine feminization, which would make of them, instead, men in disguise? Would this then constitute a progressive vision?

Relative to the question of a progressive vision, Gibson demystifies adolescent masculinity to a certain extent, and thus opens it up to the possibility of change. This occurs when it is revealed that Case's energy, his risk-taking, his thrill, and finally what gives him the power to break through the final "ice" is self-hatred. "You gotta hate somebody before this is over," the Finn's voice says (261). Case keeps trying on different kinds of hatred, but when it comes to the final moment, the motivation is self-hatred (262). This is one of the cynical and profound truths of adolescent philosophy: the way self-hatred motivates thought, feeling, and action. This self-hatred, suggests Gibson, can be used to do great things. It can be harnessed for the purposes of liberation; it is, in other words, protopolitical, if and only if it is recognized as such and channeled in a certain way.

And yet certain aspects of the text entrench it within old ideologies of nature, culture, and the body in ways that seem unable to offer an alternative to the binarisms that structure Western thought. There is a persistent nostalgia in *Neuromancer* for nature and the natural, even as the body is that which is spurned and rejected as mere "meat." This nostalgia surfaces, as I noted above, in relation to romantic love and in relation to sexual difference, not vis-à-vis Molly, but in relation to Linda, the lost and mourned love object of the novel. This is not surprising if we think of *Neuromancer* as a cultural map of the new, computer-literate, adolescent masculine psychic formation. But what does this nostalgia do? Does it keep "woman" in the realm of nature? Does it promise salvation or redemption? Does it fatally idealize and pedestalize the feminine?

Stone makes the point that cyberspace expresses a desire for "freedom from the body, freedom from the sense of loss of control that accompanies adolescent male embodiment. Cyberspace is surely also a concretization of the psychoanalytically framed desire of the male to achieve freedom" (107). She warns about the danger of forgetting about the body, and its implications for the rest of us in the virtual reality future (113). However, it is clear that cyberpunk does not eliminate the body from its representations; even the presence of being in cyberspace is marked by "icons," which stand in for bodies. Transactions, negotiations, and communication take place between and among various representatives of bodies, however differently configured they might be from what we know as the biological body.

Furthermore, *Neuromancer* figures racialization, as it does gender to a certain extent and sexuality, in ways that do not depart radically from the entrenched dichotomies of present-day social relations. Asian-ness, in the novel, is configured in terms of U.S. popular cultural fantasies of orientalism in relation to Japan. Finally, the only consistent political and theological philosophy expressed in the book is represented by the Rastafarian community (note the names: Maelcom, and his tugboat, the *Marcus Garvey*). The Rastafarians reject the company and industrial technology and adopt Case and Molly as the beings who will go into Babylon, liberate it, and usher in the new Zion. Here we see that what is Black, or "African," comes to be idealized and exoticized as that which is natural, authentic, and true, much as, Frith argues, Africa and African music function in the domain of (white) rock to lend exoticism and authenticity to its aesthetic energies.[13] Thus the rejection of the technocultural and the longing for the natural also come to be "embodied" in the most traditional (white) symbol of the natural, the primitive, and the body in Western culture.

C. The Cultural Politics of the *Alien* Films

Alien

Alien, directed by Ridley Scott (1979); *Aliens,* directed by James Cameron and produced by Gale Ann Hurd, his wife (1986); and *Alien³,* directed by David Fincher and coproduced by Sigourney Weaver (1992), can be called trickle-up horror/science fiction movies, films that have high production value, have garnered an expansive market, and thus have been treated as less disreputable than (what are called) grade B or exploitation horror movies.[14] Their hybrid genre, both horror and science fiction, makes them particularly sensitive registers of the psychic and the sociopolitical. The horror genre typically deals with (more or less unconscious) nightmares involving sexuality (specifically, sexual undifferentiation), where, as Robin Wood puts it, "normality [defined as conformity to the dominant social norms] is threatened by the Monster."[15] Horror films thus invite psychoanalytic interpretations that explore unconscious desires and fantasy. Science fiction most explicitly addresses the political, representing political fantasies through the imagining of alternative worlds, and thus invites the reading of **ideologemes,** or ideological critique.[16]

The film titles indicate an encounter with the other in its most generic form, less readily visible in films where the name of the other is "thing" or "fly." The titles also invoke nationalism: "alien" is the term used to designate those on the other side of national borders. These films, then, one might assume, deal in overt ways with questions of sexual alterity and nationalism. Furthermore, as a series that extends over thirteen years, each installment appearing in a different decade (1979, 1986, 1992), the first three *Alien* films permit a contextual as well as intertextual political/sexual reading, whereby ideologemes specific to a historical moment become more readable for being variations of the "same" story. Finally, these films have been variously taken up by feminists and queers as emblems of progressive political representation, and thus have functioned ideologically as symptoms of some of the liberal democratic dilemmas I have been exploring.

Ridley Scott's *Alien* (1979) refers to *2001* as the paradigmatic science fiction film emerging in the context of nuclear panic, and the concomitant fear that technology carries with it a moralized promise of extermination. I say "moralized" because there has always been a sense in Western cultures that the technological is fascinating, useful, helpful, and dangerous (the story of Prometheus stealing fire from the gods comes to mind). A residual guilt persists concerning the conquest of nature, as in the aphorism "It's not nice to fool Mother Nature!" or Laurie Anderson's song (and the fable from which the song's title is taken) "The Monkey's Paw," where she mockingly admonishes, "Nature's got rules and nature's got laws, and if you go too far it's the monkey's paws."[17] Is this guilt about "man's" mistreatment of Mother Nature guilt about the son's incestuous rape of Mother Nature? Given the metaphor of reproduction, one might speculate that the conquest of nature is likened to a sexual act—perhaps violent— that engenders technology. The very act of naming the computer in *Alien* "mother" (MU TH UR) suggests the displacement of birth through the need to reconstruct the mother as a product of men's brains. This imagined, artificial male birth functions to mitigate, in some sense, fears about the hostility (revenge) of the mother (Mother Nature).

Alien also quotes *2001* directly, in the embryonic birth scenes of the ship's crew, in the chamber music that plays inside the command room, in the look of the ship's computer, and especially in the scenes of Ripley's hallucinogenic orgasm as she watches *Nostromo* blow up, with the colors and shapes that are reflected on her helmet. How then, does *Alien* change the terms of *2001*?

Alien is born at an interesting moment in the United States: 1979. It is the peak, climax, or end of the second wave of the women's movement. It is also the period of the oil crisis in the United States, the beginning of the realization that the high-tech, land of plenty empire that is the United States is ruining its resources and is fatally flawed in its radical dependence on oil that is not controlled by the United States but by OPEC in the Middle East. Thus the ship is called *Nostromo* (the title of Conrad's novel that signals the dream of empire and also the decline of imperialist and colonialist Great Britain), and the ship is a refinery that transports or tows mineral ore from interplanetary space back to earth.[18] It even looks like an offshore oil rig: dirty, dark, greasy, dank, its metal oily and rusted. The ambivalence about technological progress is expressed in this image of the commercial and messy business of acquiring our most used and needed resource for the maintenance of our glossy, high-tech existence.

Sofia discusses this ambivalent representation of technology by referring to the "bad slimy by-product" that is always a consequence of our shiny new objects. (This is **repressed** or suppressed in cyberspace science fiction, which retreats from this view of technology, taking refuge in the high-tech, clean, and glossy planes of the inner technological space of the computer; although there too there is the **return of the repressed** in the form of chaotic behavior within cyberspace.) The film interestingly figures our culture's fears about technology and the nature/culture ambivalence at the heart of the discourse of better living through technology. Several figures in the movie connect its anxieties historically to the question of the oil shortage and the consequent reevaluation of U.S. economic dependence on "foreign" supplies: (1) the creature changes organic matter into inorganic matter: it transforms human blood into a kind of silicon plastic that makes a perfect protective case of the human body for the new creatures to gestate in; (2) when the crew go into the abandoned ship on the planet, they see the captain of that ship fused to the ship, and they say that he has been fossilized. The linkage of fossilization of an organic body to high tech transformations alludes to oil (the detritus of organic matter compressed into petroleum), which is then used to construct technologically advanced civilizations. Both of these images or figurations of the anxiety about technology express an ambivalent attitude toward that technology and its relationship to the human body, organic matter, or nature. Oil is, of course, the perfect metaphor for the expression of such dis-ease, because it brings together the organic and the inorganic, nature and technology.

The beginning of the film portrays humans as weak and helpless as they emerge from their womblike and dormant state inside the ship's uterine capsules. They complain. At the same time, the complaints of the mechanics of the ship, who point to the inequity of wage distribution and threaten to strike, produce a discourse about the failure of manufacturing. The movie conveys a certain despair and cynicism about industrial America and its failures to make a shiny sleek machine that works perfectly: the workers, the mechanical keys to the functioning of the entire military-industrial complex, will not cooperate (note that the film adopts the popular ideological stance that labor is to blame for the failure of industry in the United States). The humans are imperfect because, in part, they impede the smooth operation of technological efficiency and industrial growth. But the technology is imperfect too. When members of the crew go into the abandoned spaceship, the video monitor fails; MU TH UR cannot decode the warning signal; and voices speaking over the intercom sound deeply distorted.

The alien, on the other hand, is a powerful figure of the natural; and it is no accident that praise for the alien comes from a being who is an imperfect welding of the human and the technological: the cyborg Ash ("dust to dust, ashes to ashes"), who admires its perfection. "I admire its purity," he says (and we might wonder about the racial subtext here). It has a perfect defense system, it is flawless, and it is untroubled by human emotions, which always clutter up the project of rational technological progress. The alien is thus the revenge of nature: the perfect killing machine that is not a machine, the perfect organism that can make even inorganic substances become part of itself. It is both a parasite and a carnivore (we learn primarily about its reproductive functioning, another instance of Sofia's point that fantasies about technology are reproductive fantasies). And what it really excels at is reproducing itself using human bodies. *Alien* is thus a nightmare fantasy about biological reproduction, which culminates in the bizarre cesarean birth of the alien from the chest cavity of Cain (Abel's brother, and thus a scapegoat, Cain is the most "feminine" man of the crew, and he speaks with a British accent).

Ultimately *Alien*, unlike its successors, can be read as a kind of parable about the revenge of Mother Nature against mankind's audacious claim to conquer her through technological perfection, although the ending nevertheless celebrates the triumph of humanism over the alienness of nature, albeit after demonstrating technocracy's failure to do so through scientific means. The humanism that triumphs is no longer the heroic male technocrat, but a woman.

Science fiction often repeats medieval romance quest motifs—the story of the lone, heroic (but flawed) individual protagonist who must test himself against supernatural or magical natural forces that are malignant, evil, and dangerous and emerge triumphant into the world once again. Here that heroic individual is Sigourney Weaver's Ripley (note the pun on the director's name, Ridley Scott, in the character of the protagonist Ripley). *Alien* thus inscribes the women's movement into its medieval plot about the hero's conquest of the monstrous dragon.

How does this film engage the question of feminism? One could argue that Ripley is the hero for commercial reasons, that the movie industry is marketing to the "new woman" consumer, a middle-class liberal feminist professional woman. She may represent the triumph of humanistic values in the film—a feat that requires overcompensating gestures, since the film takes such delight in its antihumanistic technology: the alien and the cyborg. Furthermore, because Ripley has to be a hero, we also see the film overcompensating in its attempt to feminize her. For example, her anger and aggression are staged as a typically feminine "catfight" in the scene where she calls MU TH UR a bitch. Ash's attack on Ripley also feminizes her in that it resembles an attempted rape, and this fight brings into play the medieval motif that signals the presence of the lady—blood drops on the snow—with a twist: the blood is Ripley's and the snow is the "milk" of Ash's android-sustaining substance. The presence of Jones, Ripley's cat, as sidekick also works to feminize the heroine: there is a silent pun on "pussy," while Ripley's concern for Jones demonstrates her maternal feelings. At the same time, however, the film also pokes fun at these values, by making Ripley's attempts to save the cat border on the absurd. Finally, the confrontation between Ripley and the alien also genders her as feminine by awkwardly invoking the traditional "tits and ass" stuff of movies (she is in her underwear), likening the scene once again to a near-rape. *Alien* thus simultaneously acknowledges the appeal of the tough female/feminist heroine *and* feels some unease about it by making overcompensating gestures to return her to her "proper" gender.

Aliens

By 1986 things have changed. Hollywood films in the eighties seem to conduct a steady retreat from social commentary. In the seventies, most films commented on the social, usually in ominous tones. Nuclear destruction, vanishing resources, increasing surveillance of civilian life, multinational corporations' greed and power—such was the stuff of many films, even when the subject matter appeared to be unrelated.

In the eighties, however, the personal, the private, the individual took over with a vengeance. In some ways this development parallels the ideology or ethos Andrew Ross refers to in his discussion of New Age technocultures and New Age philosophies as voluntarist individualism, exemplified in statements like "We are participating, however unconsciously, in the process of disease," and "We can choose health instead."[19] In the eighties social disorders are likened to illnesses brought on in part by the victims of those illnesses themselves. According to Ross,

> When personal consciousness is the single determining factor in social change, then all social problems, including the specters raised by racism, imperialism, sexism, and homophobia, are seen as the result of personal failures and shortcomings. Individual consciousness becomes the source, rather than a major site of socially oppressive structures, and opportunities for a radical humanism are lost. ("New Age Technoculture," 546)

This description of New Age philosophies could apply in many ways to the mainstream descriptions we hear about phenomena such as racism, sexism, homophobia, poverty, and violence, and illustrates how much New Age thinking has become part of the mainstream social outlook of the eighties.

Films of the eighties, by and large, subscribe to these forms of individualism and voluntarism. Whereas *Alien* was centrally and anxiously about technophilia, the destruction wrought on the world by corporate greed and unrestrained technofetishism, and the unlikelihood of a redemptive humanism that would restore the ecosystem, *Aliens* is untroubled by earthly pollution or the power of technology's reign. Instead there is an adoration of technology at work and a more thorough recognition that the boundaries between nature and technology, between biology and technology, have been definitively blurred (in the way that both Haraway and Ross talk about).[20] Like Gibson's

Neuromancer, *Aliens* recognizes that there is no going back and that it is ultimately impossible to separate the technological from the humanistic or the natural.

Alien was horrified by the blurring of the boundaries between nature and technology, further suggesting that nature might actually win out in the end in revenge for humanity's audacity at having dreamed that technology would bring transcendence. *Alien* constructed an opposition between the technological and the biological, the technological and the natural. *Aliens*, instead, revels in the technological and in the cyborg mix of human and machine. As spectators of the film, we often look through video monitors (with the names of the "bio beings" displayed in the lower left-hand corner of the screen). Whereas in the first film we witnessed the failure of the monitors when the crew entered the alien spacecraft where the creature was living, here there are glitches (as when Drake has to adjust his monitor, and when it temporarily stops working inside the incubation room), but for the most part, technology works beautifully. In addition, we learn that the marines are dead when their monitors stop working and display television "snow" (a reconception of death as a blank [but turned on] TV screen); thus technology becomes the primary—and reliable—source of knowledge. This use of video must also be commenting on the medium of film itself, here no longer ambivalently regarded as a technology that threatens the human director's supremacy over his product. In *Aliens*, it would seem, director and camera meld into one smooth and invisible visual field, uninterrupted by quirky shots that draw attention to the virtuosity of a director/"artiste" behind the scene.

This use of video monitoring also says something about the perfection of technological surveillance mechanisms in the eighties. Whereas *Alien* was anxious about surveillance tactics, *Aliens* assumes their existence and, indeed, sides with the technological optimism of the military. Paul Virilio observes that *Aliens* celebrates high-tech military weaponry; indeed, after the Gulf War, this film resembles nothing so much as a proleptic television commercial for the war (including what could be called the new gender equality of the military; this film even looks forward to the time when it will be acceptable for gays to be in the military).[21]

Technophilia abounds in *Aliens:* the android, Bishop, is a good guy; the cargoloader, Ripley's metallic armature, is a good thing; the marines are armed with state-of-the-art weapons that function efficiently. The spaceship is brighter and cleaner; it has everything, and even though the crew still complains about the food, it is clear that this is a more comfortable ride than the *Nostromo*. What causes damage to people is not so much the malfunctioning of the machines as the deliberate corruption of the CIA-like company, whose disregard for human life has reached new heights of diabolical intensity. There are some technological failures, of course, and these primarily concern the eighties' recognition of nuclear power plants as faulty technology (yet there is still an optimism that they can be fixed): the plant as a whole has problems that will result in a nuclear reaction, but Bishop (the android) and the others can solve them. There is a final meltdown of the plant, recalling once again the ultimate threat of nuclear power plants, but the film reworks its significance so that the meltdown turns out to be beneficial rather than harmful.

I said that *Aliens*, like many films of the eighties, moves away from social commentary into the realm of the personal, the private, the individual. This is a story about a domestic quarrel, not between husband and wife or parent and child, but between two women, two mothers. The motivating force of the film now comes from Ripley's single-minded rage against the aliens and her desire to destroy them. The fiction used to personalize this rage is the fiction of maternal ferocity, the fabled notion that a mother will do anything and everything to protect her young. Indeed, there are moments in the film where Ripley's disregard for the lives and safety of the crew members is striking in comparison with her obsessive and single-minded concern for her adoptive "daughter," Newt. Rather than a kind of protofeminist humanism, as was displayed in *Alien*, what characterizes Ripley in *Aliens* is a private, personal, and selfish concern for one being: the girl. *Aliens* thus becomes a story about maternal jealousy. There is a link between the maternal feminine—or the virile feminine as maternal—portrayed here and the discourse of nationalism, for in the discourse of nationalism, women are primarily and positively constructed as ferocious and protective mothers.

It is precisely around questions of nationalism and imperialism that the film's ideological confusion seems most apparent and works to enshrine political denial. What is the political situation on the planet where Ripley, Burke, Bishop, and the marines go to inspect the colony? We learn that a colony of "terraformers" has settled there; earth has colonized this planet, and, in an apt metaphor, is proceeding to transform its "hostile" atmosphere into one that will be terra-friendly. The colonists tame the wilderness, transforming the "uninhabitable" land into one that will host its terraform settlers with ease and comfort. In the interrogation scene where Ripley is asked to report to the company about what she knows of the planet, the female scientist says to Ripley, "You're telling us that there is this indigenous alien life form there that has been totally unrecorded and unnoticed?" Ripley, at this point, hyperbolically stresses that the life form is not indigenous; in fact, she ridicules the woman for her stupidity (notice that there are many hostile exchanges between Ripley and other women in this movie, and that these hostile exchanges are always at the expense of the other woman in the encounter, another indication that this movie is replete with backlash). The aliens arrived, supposedly, in an alien spaceship; that is where they were originally found. This alien spaceship, which, in the first movie, looked like the ruins of some kind of ancient civilization, arrived on the planet before the terraformers settled their colony there, and thus the aliens are not indigenous to the planet, which is terribly important in Ripley's view.

This argument sounds like nothing so much as the self-justifying rhetoric of imperialist or colonial ventures. There is both an argument about who has the right to settle on land and a defensive argument about how no one is indigenous to that land. No one has a prior, more compelling claim, and therefore the colonists have a right to colonize it and to settle there. (Here the motif of cannibalism associated with the aliens is probably more tightly linked to the political unconscious of the film text than it was in the first film, in the sense that the rhetoric of the film evokes arguments for the colonization of the Americas as well.) This argument conceals what might otherwise seem obvious in this film: that the aliens have destroyed the human terraformers who invaded their planet and restored it to its "rightful" occupants, the aliens, who were there first.

This is the structural situation that persists throughout the movie and is also continually denied: the alien is fighting for survival against an enemy, humanity, that wants to destroy it and its offspring. Ripley and the marines (is the use of the marines a sign of bad conscience about Vietnam, Grenada, or Nicaragua?) are involved in a genocidal campaign against these aliens, who fight back in order to survive as a species. And how does one fight back? Kill the mother! Ripley is the one who starts the war to decide whose offspring dies, when she maliciously—we see the glint in her eye—torches the mother alien's eggs and then her eggsac. It is only after this offensive maneuver that the mother alien goes after Ripley and also after Ripley's adoptive daughter. Geopolitics is translated into a drama about two mothers fighting over the respective lives of their offspring. The future of the globe is transformed into a deadly battle between two women, two mothers duking it out over whose kids get to live. This is what I mean by the personalization of the social, the individualizing of the political in the eighties.

Aliens is replete with bad faith. Under the guise of feminism and multiculturalism, the film enacts intense backlash and antifeminism.[22] First, it displaces geopolitics onto a catfight (interesting that Jones disappears in this film). The women are the problem in this story; they are the truly fierce ones of the species. However, *Aliens* seems feminist on the surface, and has become a cult film among feminists and lesbians. It seems to portray lesbians in quite a favorable light (the medic, Ferro, and Vasquez), although, of course, the marine Vasquez has to "be" a man (and a woman of color, who can thus be more easily masculinized in popular culture representations than a white woman). Some might argue that there is no explicit indication of lesbianism, but I think the film inserts recognition codes that signal to its subcultural audience that the women are lesbians. Recognition codes are, of course, stereotypical, and so you have the short hair, the musculature, the joke about being a man, and the bonding between Vasquez and Ferro.[23]

Ripley is tougher in this film than she was in *Alien* (she has shorter hair; in *Alien³* her head is shaved). She is a macho female hero, and her bonding with Hicks turns out to resemble more of a brotherhood than a marriage, though the nuclear family does, nevertheless, get reconstructed through mutual and equal admiration between "husband" and "wife": there is the joke about the tracking bracelet that Hicks gives to Ripley as a mock gift, which seems to poke fun at heterosexual bonding arrangements. Ripley, in turn, gives the bracelet to Newt, thus cementing the familial bond. The director's restored version of the film seems anxious about the feminism and the lesbianism of the film, because scenes have been inserted that bring it into line with a kind of compulsory heterosexuality. Ripley is excessively maternalized and thus feminized: we find out that she had a biological daughter. (Being female in this film is primarily about motherhood; is this related to the abortion debate?) Meanwhile, a scene is inserted where Hicks and Ripley exchange first names, which also further genders Ripley—now Ellen—as feminine and "straight."

On the surface, the film appears to be feminist, even as it seems to be anxious about that appearance. Elsewhere, however, the message moves in another direction. The bad guy is a woman too, and a mother. The scenes of hostile confrontation between Ripley and other women—culminating in the gratuitous "Get away from her, you bitch!"—seem to say that the only way one can have a feminist woman is if she is a lone individual heroine who explicitly does not bond with other women.

What are the racial politics of the film? Vasquez dies a noble death the way Parker did in *Alien*, invoking the theme of ultimate self-sacrifice as the mark of "good" people of color in the nation. One indicator that racial politics is indeed at issue in *Aliens* is the moment when Ferro says to Vasquez, "Hey, *mira*, who's Snow White?" Racialism and racial hostilities in this film also take place in the domain of the feminine; they are seen as hostilities between women. Here again we have the phenomenon of class conflict (or racial conflict) being figured as an attack on women of the upper class, a displacement of the problems of racial strife away from men and onto women.[24]

The complex ideological contradictoriness of the film reveals itself on the terrain of race as well as gender. There is the admission that people of color, white women, and working-class white men are the ones who have to go into the military and perform on the front lines, place themselves in harm's way. As Sister Souljah puts it, this nation economically forces Black people to go into the military in order to go overseas and kill "other black people" for the United States; here the "aliens" are recruited to go out and destroy the alien ("she thought they said illegal aliens and signed up," says Hudson, the "insensitive white guy," of Vasquez). The compensation for being among those who have to die for the nation is the nation's recognition of Black patriotism. Economic necessity is reinterpreted as fervent loyalty and as the enlightened race politics of the Marine Corps. Perhaps the most pernicious, because "concealed," race politics of the movie involves the use of "alien" to mean both xenomorph and "immigrant" (e.g., the comment about "illegal aliens"; the quips in Spanish, as when the sergeant calls the marines "tough hombres" and Vasquez's Spanish motto; the processing center, which is reminiscent of the U.S./Mexico border). In addition, the comparison between Ripley and the alien mother suggests a racialized discourse of motherhood that centers this time on the infamous ideological image of the "welfare queen": the bad (black) alien mother lays tons of eggs, creates teeming masses of baby aliens that will take over the world by devouring the rest of us, while the good white mom has just one—adopted—child.

Finally, the android situation in this movie seems to comment on the perceived state of white masculinity in the culture. Why does the film wound the male hero and make the android Bishop the co-rescuer with Ripley? Bishop, the only truly good and competent man in the film, is not a man at all, but an artificial person (note that the film plays on political correctness with the scene where Bishop asks to be called an artificial person rather than an android). *Aliens* seems to suggest that the only good man, the only kind that can be counted on, is an android. This situation, and the staging of the drama of rival mothers, as well as the drama of the mother/daughter bond, are the signs that *Aliens* is trying in some deep ways to connect with the American middle-class female (and feminist) psyche, that is, to recognize and acknowledge her fears, concerns, and anxieties. In this sense the film caters to a female audience and shows the extent to which the cultural imagination has grasped some notions of women's discontent in America, although I think it is important to remember that discourses of nationalism (and this film is, I would argue, quite a rabid discourse of nationalism) always pass, both metaphorically and literally, through the figure and person of motherhood, mothers, and the maternal.

Alien³

After such a frightening and brilliant construction of the "illusion of a seamless reality" that indicates "the potential allure, power, invisibility of humanist ideological semes" ("even for the radical critic," notes James Kavanaugh, 99), I can only rejoice that David Fincher ended up directing *Alien³*, with Sigourney Weaver as coproducer.[25] If *Alien* can be said to have interpellated (primarily) a straight male spectatorship, and *Aliens* extended that interpellation to include most markedly a straight female, feminist, and lesbian spectatorship, then *Alien³*, I would argue, reaches most markedly toward a gay male spectator. I want to conduct a tentative defense of this movie for several reasons: it was a box office flop, too depressing. The cheery eighties film-goers were unprepared to see the mood of the turn of the decade reflected before their eyes: economic disaster, AIDS, the end of the Reagan-Bush era, wars in Europe, the Gulf War, the Clarence Thomas hearings, and the approaching millennium. The beginning of 1992 was not a happy time. The film does not have a happy ending. It is, politically, an improvement. Furthermore, the film is directed by a video director, a relative outsider in the industry whose traffic in the more pedestrian, populist medium of video makes him the object of many film directors' scorn. And, finally, with its algorithmic marker as the third in the series, *Alien³* critically suggests the infinite exponentiality of the othering we are capable of, while killing off this particular series of sequels by obliterating its protagonist.[26]

Reviewers have pointed out that *Alien³* is obviously about AIDS.[27] My students have remarked, however, that this is equally if not more true of the second film, and there the absolutely alien as contagion (from elsewhere) is horrifying, terrible, threatening to the rest of us, the good, innocent ones. In the second film, whether intentional or not, the discourse of AIDS proliferates in its most homophobic form. In *Alien³*, such is not the case. If AIDS is among us, it is among all of us, and what it produces as reaction is not so much horror as sorrow.

The film takes place on Fiorina ("Fury") 161, a YY chromosome work correctional facility.[28] There are twenty-five male prisoners who remain there voluntarily, since Weyland-Yutani's mineral ore refinery no longer functions. They are bound together by an "apocalyptic millenarian Christian fundamentalism," according to Clemens, the doctor, and they have taken a vow of celibacy ("and that includes women," says one of the men). They all have shaved heads and wear punkish fatigues and boots. Clemens is an ex-junkie who still "fetishizes the ritual," for we see him lovingly shoot up Ripley twice in the space of fifteen minutes. These, along with some lines of dialogue and what Amy Taubin points out is a relentless foregrounding and probing of the body, set up the AIDS discourse in the film.[29]

There is a Foucauldian cast to the description of this social order. The YY also signals this discursive encoding, for a medicalized link has been made between identity (symbolized by the biological reference, YY) and criminal behavior. The planet is a bathhouse, a hospital, and a prison, a company prison at that, suggesting a total melding of state and capital in this new world order. The phrases initially used to describe the problem of contagion—"in the interest of public health," "communicable infection," and "unwelcome virus"—signal the discursive technologies of medicine and the state, while an autopsy performed on Newt early in the film visually reinforces those discursive technologies. Against this backdrop, the film introduces us to a group of outcasts: male criminals, an ex-junkie doctor, and a sole surviving flight officer who is also the only woman on the planet. The film also elaborates a discourse of resistance around these characters, a populist *bricolage* of religious fundamentalism and political analysis. Several lines in the movie signal this resistance as belonging to communities of activism such as ACT UP: "They think we're crud and they don't give a fuck about one friend of yours that's died!" says Ripley. Funeral rites are ceremonialized and turned into community rituals replete with significance. The film foregrounds community: the group is what counts, not the lone individual, for the nature of the problem is such that only the group members' commitment to each other will solve it.[30] There is no "proper" leader, either, for the doctor and the jailer (as the state's proxy) are killed off early on. Ripley becomes nominal leader, but only nominal, and

Dillon (Charles Dutton), the spiritual leader of the group, firmly refuses the role.

Alien³ elaborates a discourse of AIDS, ACT UP resistance, and gay community that is queer-sympathetic, to a certain degree. The most powerful argument for the film's gay sympathies is suggested by Stephen Scobie, who argues that the deeply elegiac tone and mood of this film stem from its elaboration of the mourning produced by survivor's guilt.[31] He reads the guilt as Ripley's, and the mourning as maternal and centered specifically on Newt, but it does not take much to extend the sense of this mourning so that it simultaneously speaks to the mourning of gay men for their friends and lovers, mothers for their sons, activist sisters for their brothers, and the survivor's guilt an entire community might share.

Unlike a discourse of nationalism, which would heroize the surviving mother's mourning for her war-destroyed sons, *Alien³* reworks the image of pregnancy to signal, instead, **incorporation**, the failure of the mourner's **introjection**, which would assimilate the death of the loved one into the ongoing life of the mourner. Scobie, following Abraham and Torok, points out that "incorporation is at once more drastic and more paradoxical, in that the 'other' which is assimilated remains other" (88).[32] This incorporation of a queen, another mother, and the suicide that will destroy both the mourner and the doppelgänger within shut off the future and condemn it. There is no redemption for *Alien³*. Death produces not future life (as we are told it does by the nation-states that send us to war and that attempt to console the rest of us for our losses), but the end of the story. The final scene in the film is deeply ironic: a roll call of the recorded voice of Ripley and text on the screen tell the viewer that the planet was sealed. Ripley's death is all the more ironic for being futile: she does not destroy the company. One of the reasons, then, that audiences found this film depressing is precisely this exposure of the production of death as cruel, involuntary, and senseless. As Taubin remarks, "More pessimistic and unsparing than *Thelma and Louise*, Fincher's *Alien³* suggests that Ripley knows that the odds are against there being anyone left in the world for whom her myth will have meaning" (10).

But what of Dillon, the Parker-Vasquez sacrificial heroic Black character of this version of the alien allegory? Like Parker and Brett in

Alien, he refuses the humanistic role offered him when Ripley tries to make friendly contact. He refuses, in other words, to be rescripted as sacrificial humanist by insisting, when questioned by Ripley, that he is "a murderer and a rapist of women." The couple Dillon/Ripley in this film resembles, finally, the partnership Vasquez/Drake of *Aliens*: a heroic, ironic, unsentimentalized, nonsexual (but erotic) partnership of outcast comrades. We might, nevertheless, ask whether the narrative logic of the film ultimately appropriates Dillon for the humanist cause, because he too finally goes the way of Parker and Vasquez, a good Black man who heroically sacrifices himself for the community by keeping the alien penned where it can be killed off.[33]

Ripley asks, in fact, that Dillon kill her, presuming him capable, given his former career. Another logic, more unsettling, appears in this moment of would-be heroic sacrifice. When Dillon and Ripley trap the alien—which, in this film, is lifted out of the discourse of anthropomorphic sexual difference by being born of a dog—in the lead mold, they argue about who will stay to die as the hot lead falls. Ripley says, "I'm staying—I want to die," but Dillon says they made a deal that he would kill her later on. She climbs out of the mold but he remains there. She says, "What about me?" and he responds, "God'll take care of you now, sister," thus breaking the promise he had just invoked to her in order to achieve his own *jouissance* in death-grappling with the other. Could this doubly negative gesture be doubly ironic, and thus critical of the sacrificial narrative set up in the previous two films? Rather than the redemption of the racial/sexual outcast through heroic self-sacrifice in the service of the preservation of the nation (figured as white womanhood), the scene mimes the sacrificial act but ironizes it by making it a refusal to "save" the woman. However, "saving" her also involves killing her, so the refusal is also a refusal of the typical (negative) role assigned to the racial outcast. A second irony involves the turning of "sacrifice" into **narcissism**, in that Dillon chooses his own desire over the wishes of Ripley. But that narcissism also involves suicide. Choosing himself means killing himself, just as choosing her would have meant killing her. Thus Dillon redeems himself from the taint of "rapist and murderer of women," but not for the sake of another. The question, then, might be, is it possible to reconfigure the meaning of redemptive self-sacrifice such that it does not shore up the nation? This question becomes also a question about whether it is ever possible to valorize the death drive as oppositional resistance.[34]

If we read this as a film about survivor's guilt, then indeed it is no wonder it did not bring audiences rushing to it, for how can one simply come to the conclusion that willed death, suicide, might be what the subject desires? Is this not then the film's humanist weakness as well, its existentialist solution to overwhelming odds? (Dillon's message to the reluctant prisoners is "You're all gonna die, the only question is how you're gonna check out. . . . Do you want it on your feet or on your knees, begging?") Could one not imagine leaving the monster as legacy behind for the company to discover and deal with? Would this not constitute a means of fighting back? This would perhaps be the only message more horrifying to its audience than the spectacle of Ripley's demise. The deaths of the prisoners, however futile, confer upon them honor and dignity, and thus redeem them, if not the world. The eerie roll-call roster at the end of the film that reads like the names of the dead at the Names Project exhibitions does just this, and does what the Names recital does as well: heroizes the dead for those who have lost them and confers dignity and honor on their lives. The conferral of such dignity, and anger at the company that is the cause of all this slaughter, may thus elicit our humanist sympathies for a film whose message also includes an incitement to bash Japan, for the barrels in the basement of the facility are covered in Japanese writing, and the scientist who accompanies the company representative at the end of the film is Japanese.

And yet a metatextual moment governs this film, performs a **mise-en-abîme** via an ironic allusion to the genre of horror films. When she discovers that she is carrying an alien fetus, Ripley decides to go find the (adult) alien. The assistant warden asks her where it is; she says, "It's just down there, in the basement." He replies, "This whole place is a basement," to which Ripley responds, "It's a metaphor," signaling the genre of horror as that which talks about "the thing in the basement." But then she does descend to the basement, to the dream place, to the unconscious, and literally enacts the moment of misrecognition psychoanalysis accords to such confrontations. In what is the most moving, **uncanny**, and sexy speech of the entire film, she says to the alien, "Where are you when I need you?" and, picking up a pipe as she hunts it down, "Don't be afraid, I'm part of the family." As she thinks she sees it cowering on the floor, she says, "You've been in my life so long, I can't remember anything else. Now do something for me. It's easy, just do what you do." At this point she brings the pipe crashing down, only to discover that she has hit another pipe, and not the creature, who is hiding in the rafters.[35] Is Ripley here speaking to the alien, to herself? Is this Sigourney speaking to the alien, to us, her audience of thirteen years? And what is she saying? The seduction, the intimacy, the desire of this moment, its uncanny elegiac resonances seem to move it out of the absurd and rather ridiculous space of a woman talking to a creature that does not understand and may not even be there. Might the "you" be death itself? The death of Sigourney Weaver as Ripley, principal character of the *Alien* trilogy? The signing-off not only of Ripley, last surviving officer of the *Nostromo*, but also of Weaver herself? And is the desire uncanny because, while we all know that the literal death is a metaphorical one, it also speaks to a desire for death as other, as alien, in the space of the basement, the topographical space of the unconscious?

The film thus explores the subject's death drive, explores desire as the desire to die. And it marks the subject's relation to the social (the company and the loss of others) as resistance and refusal: "no" is repeated several dramatic times toward the end. In the penultimate scene the sole survivor turns around, as he is being herded out, for one last look at the prison and begins to laugh. The company men shove him out and he retorts, "Fuck you." What this film leaves its survivors (viewers) with is a space for mourning.

Recent psychoanalytic discussions of AIDS and "homo-sex" suggest that a rejection of the "culture of redemption" (Leo Bersani's phrase) and the valorization of the death drive might constitute an oppositional negativity that is not so much antihumanist as posthumanist in its critique.[36] Tim Dean has suggested that the theorization of the death drive as the (homosexual) *jouissance* of the Other—"that death itself is actually something one might, at some radical level, want—if not desire" (105)—makes possible the project of a "cure for sociosymbolic ills" (115) around the question of our culture's response to AIDS. Dean's bold if problematic formulation of his argument that "in a psychotic society we are all PWAs" (116) may have found a figure in this film.[37] I want to suggest that *Alien³* may at least offer a way of imagining resistance (as absolute refusal) to a narrative of redemption that valorizes self-sacrifice for the good of the nation and that attempts to enlist outcast recruits for a national project of imperialism.[38]

Cultural Studies and Popular Culture

Sample Syllabus

What is cultural studies and why is it all the rage? Through an examination of both critical essays and primary texts of popular or mass culture productions, such as Madonna, pornography, rap, MTV, and film, this course will explore the discipline called cultural studies as it has been newly constituted in the United States. What are the reasons for its emergence? What are its politics? How does cultural studies bridge the gap between the academic and the popular? Can cultural studies help us understand the explosion of mass media in the United States and its domestic and global significance? These are some of the questions we will be exploring in our study of a variety of texts in several media.

Required Texts

C. Freccero, *Popular Culture: An Introduction*
L. Grossberg et al., *Cultural Studies*
M. Nava, *How Town*
O. Butler, *Dawn*
J. Gomez, *The Gilda Stories*
S. Schulman, *People in Trouble*
S. Cisneros, *Woman Hollering Creek*
b. hooks, *Yearning*
W. Gibson, *Neuromancer*
Los Bros Hernandez, *Heartbreak Soup and Other Stories*
——, *Flies on the Ceiling*

Recommended

G. Turner, *British Cultural Studies: An Introduction*
Los Bros Hernandez, *Love and Rockets: Short Stories*
D. Hebdige, *Subculture*

Week 1. Introduction to Cultural Studies

Freccero, *Popular Culture*, chaps. 1, 2A; Grossberg et al., *Cultural Studies*, chap. 5 (Brunt); chap. 10 (Fiske).
FILM: *Dressed to Kill*
RECOMMENDED: Turner, *British Cultural Studies*, pt. I, chaps. 1–2.

Week 2. Serial Killers and American Culture

hooks, *Yearning*, chaps. 1, 2, 3, 13; Freccero, *Popular Culture*, chap. 2B; Halberstam, "Skinflick: Posthuman Gender in Jonathan Demme's *The Silence of the Lambs*," *Camera Obscura* 27 (September 1991): 37–52; Young, "*The Silence of the Lambs* and the Flaying of Feminist Theory," *Camera Obscura* 27 (September 1991): 5–35.
FILM: *The Silence of the Lambs*
RECOMMENDED: Turner, *British Cultural Studies,* pt. 2, chap. 3; Grossberg et al., *Cultural Studies*, chap. 1 (Intro); chap. 7 (Clifford).

Week 3. Sexual Subcultures

Gomez, *The Gilda Stories* (entire); Freccero, *Popular Culture*, chap. 3A, B; Case, "Tracking the Vampire," *Differences: A Journal of Feminist Cultural Studies* 3, no. 2 (summer 1991): 1–20; Grossberg et al., *Cultural Studies*, chap. 18 (Haraway).
FILM: *Basic Instinct*

Week 4. Sexual Subcultures (continued)

Freccero, *Popular Culture*, chap. 3C, D; hooks, *Yearning*, 8; Grossberg et al., *Cultural Studies*, chap. 21 (Kipnis); chap. 36 (Wallace); hooks, "Madonna: Plantation Mistress or Soul Sister?" *Black Looks: Race and Representation*, 157–64; Harris, "Make My Rainy Day," *Nation*, 8 June 1992, 790–93; Freccero, "Our Lady of MTV: Madonna's 'Like a Prayer,'" *Femi-*

nism and Postmodernism, ed. Margaret Ferguson and Jennifer Wicke, 163–83.
FILM: *Truth or Dare*
RECOMMENDED: Turner, *British Cultural Studies,* pt. 2, chap. 4, pp. 158–68.

Week 5. (Re)Imagining Race, Gender, Postcoloniality

Freccero, *Popular Culture,* chap. 4A; hooks, "Is Paris Burning?" *Black Looks: Race and Representation,* 145–56; Stevens, "Love and Rockets," *Out/Look,* spring 1992, 32–33; Hernandez, *Heartbreak Soup; Flies on the Ceiling.*
FILMS: *Paris is Burning; Tongues Untied*
RECOMMENDED: hooks, *Yearning,* chap. 20; Hernandez, *Love and Rockets.*

Week 6. (Re)Imagining (continued)

Freccero, *Popular Culture,* chap. 5; Cisneros, *Woman Hollering Creek* (entire); Grossberg et al., *Cultural Studies,* chap. 6 (Chabram-Dernersesian); chap. 11 (Frith); chap. 19 (hooks); hooks, *Yearning,* chap. 18.
VIDEO: *Rap City Rhapsody*
FILM: *Do the Right Thing*
RECOMMENDED: Turner, *British Cultural Studies,* pt. 2, chap. 5.

Week 7. (Re)Imagining (continued)

Nava, *How Town* (entire); hooks, *Yearning,* chap. 16.
FILM: *Sammy and Rosie Get Laid*
RECOMMENDED: Grossberg et al., *Cultural Studies,* chaps. 4 (Bhabha), 24 (Mercer).

Week 8. Technocultures

Freccero, *Popular Culture,* chaps. 4B, C, 6A; Butler, *Dawn* (entire); Haraway, *Simians, Cyborgs, and Women: The Reinvention of Nature* (selections); Grossberg et al., *Cultural Studies,* chap. 26 (Penley); Sofia, "Exterminating Fetuses: Abortion, Disarmament, and the Sexo-Semiotics of Extraterrestrialism," *Diacritics* 14, no. 2 (summer 1984): 47–59.
FILM: *Alien*

See *Blade Runner,* Dir. Ridley Scott

Week 9. Technocultures (continued)

Freccero, *Popular Culture*, chap. 6C; Bruno, "Ramble City: Postmodernism and *Blade Runner*," *October* 41 (summer 1987): 61–74; Marder, "*Blade Runner*'s Moving Still," *Camera Obscura* 27 (September 1991): 89–107.

FILM: *Aliens*

RECOMMENDED: Turner, *British Cultural Studies*, chap. 6; Grossberg et al., *Cultural Studies*, chap. 37 (Warner).

Read either Gibson, *Neuromancer*; or Schulman, *People in Trouble*

Week 10. The Present, the Future: Dystopias

Freccero, *Popular Culture*, chap. 6B; Grossberg et al., *Cultural Studies*, chap. 8 (Crimp); chap. 15 (Grover); Stone, "Will the Real Body Please Stand Up? Boundary Stories about Virtual Cultures," *Cyberspace: First Steps*, ed. Michael Benedikt, 81–118.

FILM: *Alien³*

RECOMMENDED: Turner, *British Cultural Studies*, conclusion; Schulman, "AIDS and Homelessness," *Nation*, 10 April 1989, 480–82.

NOTES

Notes to Chapter 1

1. Certainly there are significant differences between popular culture and mass media. Graeme Turner attributes to Stuart Hall and Paddy Whannel the "influential distinction between popular art (which derives from folk cultures) and mass art (which does not): 'The typical "art" of the mass media today is not a continuity from, but a corruption of, popular art,' they say. 'Mass art has no personal quality but, instead, a high degree of personalisation.'" See Turner, *British Cultural Studies*, 2d ed., 68. He is quoting from Hall and Whannel, *The Popular Arts*.

2. See the response to Bloom and Hirsch represented by Simonson and Walker, *The Graywolf Annual Five*.

3. See Vickers, "Vital Signs: Petrarch and Popular Culture."

4. See Turner, *British Cultural Studies*, for a more thorough survey of the fields involved in cultural studies.

5. For an interesting perspective on the way the sixties shape the youth culture referred to as Generation X, see Rushkoff, *The GenX Reader*:

> As it is commonly understood today, Generation X refers to what can be called a "lost" segment of America's youth too young to remember the assassination of President Kennedy and too old to have missed the end of disco. Having watched our immediate elders transform from hippies to Yuppies to New Agers to landowners, we get the feeling we are living in the wake of the postwar baby boom and bearing the economic and cultural burden of a society run on financial credit and social debit. (3)

6. Will, "Slamming the Doors," 65.

7. See Freccero, "Our Lady of MTV: Madonna's 'Like a Prayer,'" 164, 183. My approach owes a debt of influence to Ross's *No Respect: Intellectuals and Popular Culture*; see also Ross, "Hacking Away at the Counterculture."

8. Spike Lee's *Do the Right Thing* and Madonna's work are harder to classify according to this somewhat artificial distinction between "mass" and "popular." To a certain extent, they can be viewed as inhabiting a zone between, for their

energies are often oppositional even as their work falls squarely within mainstream capitalist systems of production and distribution.

9. *Alien: Resurrection* (1997), the fourth in the series, appeared after this book was finished. It takes the themes of the first three films to the extreme of collapsing, definitively, the distinction between human and other in a vision of the posthuman inheritor of a post-technocultural (i.e., "natural") earth.

10. On pleasure, see, among others, Fradenburg and Freccero, "Caxton, Foucault, and the Pleasures of History," in *Premodern Sexualities*.

11. Žižek, "Eastern Europe's Republics of Gilead." See also *Enjoy Your Symptom*, and *Looking Awry*.

Notes to Chapter 2

1. See Turner, "The British Tradition: A Short History," in *British Cultural Studies*, 38–77.

My text is informed by two books about cultural studies that have helped shape the discipline as it is understood in humanities departments in the United States. The first, Graeme Turner's *British Cultural Studies: An Introduction*, provides a brief history of British cultural studies, a useful survey of the key concepts and central categories in cultural studies, and a discussion of the wide variety of approaches and disciplines within which cultural studies is practiced and through which the field itself has been developed. The second is *Cultural Studies*, an anthology of essays edited by Lawrence Grossberg, Cary Nelson, and Paula Treichler that grew out of an international conference, "Cultural Studies Now and in the Future," held at the University of Illinois in 1990.

2. See Turner, introduction to *British Cultural Studies*, 1–7.

3. Hebdige, *Subculture: The Meaning of Style*, 1–19.

4. See Hall, "Cultural Studies and Its Theoretical Legacies," 277–94.

5. Wallace, "Negative Images," 660.

6. I use the term "Black" (capitalized) as a political designator for the "racial" group referred to as African American, and I use the latter term when I am talking about that group in a descriptive fashion. I use "black," alternatively, to refer to a color.

7. Hall, in "Encoding and Decoding," talks about dominant (or "preferred"), negotiated, and oppositional readings of texts; these three positions that readers and/or audiences may occupy can also be said to characterize certain texts themselves.

8. Hall, "Cultural Studies," 285.

9. hooks, "Liberation Scenes," in *Yearning*, 6.

10. Althusser, "Ideology and Ideological State Apparatuses," in *Lenin and Philosophy*, 173. See also Turner, "Marxism and Ideology," in *British Cultural Studies*, 22–26, esp. 24: "Althusser's definition sees ideology not as false but as a conceptual framework 'through which men interpret, make sense of, experience and "live" the material conditions in which they find themselves' (Hall 1980a, 33). Ideology forms and shapes our consciousness of reality. For good or ill, the world it constructs is the one we will always inhabit."

11. Young, "*The Silence of the Lambs*," 7.

12. Foucault, *The History of Sexuality*. See pt. 4, "The Deployment of Sexuality," 75–80; pt. 5, "Death and Power over Life," 133–59. See also, among others, Butler, *Bodies That Matter*; Freccero, "Bodies and Pleasures: Early Modern Interrogations."

13. See also Young, "*The Silence of the Lambs.*"

14. On Rousseau, see Kaplan, *Sea Changes*, esp. "Wild Nights: Pleasure/Sexuality/Feminism," 31–56; also Freccero, "Notes of a Post–Sex Wars Theorizer."

15. For the influence of Antonio Gramsci on cultural studies, see Turner, "The Turn to Gramsci," in *British Cultural Studies*, 2d ed., 193–98.

16. hooks, "Liberation Scenes," 1–13; also "Culture to Culture," in *Yearning*, 123–33. Wallace, "Introduction: Negative/Positive Images," in *Invisibility Blues*, 1–17; also "Entertainment Tomorrow," 111–15.

17. Hall, "Cultural Studies," 286, 292. This is also discussed in the editors' introduction to Grossberg, Nelson, and Treichler, *Cultural Studies*, 10.

18. Bill Clinton made this comment during a campaign speech on June 13, 1992.

19. See Brown, "Toward a Genealogy of Moralism," for an excellent argument in favor of preserving the "critical reflection" space of the university, rather than treating universities as places where all thought is immediately translated into political action.

20. Taubin, "Killing Men (Serial Killers in Motion Pictures)," 16.

21. See Longino and Hammonds, "Conflicts and Tensions in the Feminist Study of Gender and Science," 164–83. See also Keller, *Reflections on Gender and Science*; and Schiebinger, *The Mind Has No Sex?*

22. Marx, *Capital*, vol. 1, 169–77, 486–91.

23. Privacy, a related concept, also atomizes social existence by saying there is something called the private and something called the public and that they can be separated; there are private liberties and public restrictions on freedom; private property and public property; the "private" family and "public" government or politics.

24. For a more developed analysis of the disavowal of the historical and social dimensions of violence, see Butler, "Burning Acts"; and Freccero, "Historical Violence, Censorship, and the Serial Killer."

Notes to Chapter 3

1. See Freccero, "Notes of a Post–Sex Wars Theorizer," sec. 8, "Political Agendas," 318, for the text of the Helms amendment.

2. Atwood, *The Handmaid's Tale*, 24.

3. For a more extended discussion of this issue, see Freccero, "Notes of a Post–Sex Wars Theorizer." See also Brown, *States of Injury*, particularly for its focus on the political rhetoric and strategies of Catharine MacKinnon.

4. See Weeks, *Sexuality and Its Discontents*, esp. "The New Moralism," 33–57, and "The Meaning of Diversity," 211–45.

5. See Goldberg, *Reclaiming Sodom*, 117–42, for the texts of *Bowers v. Hardwick*.

6. On sex workers' struggles and demands, see the bibliographical notes in Freccero, "Notes of a Post–Sex Wars Theorizer." In particular, see Bell, *Good Girls/Bad Girls*; and Delacoste and Alexander, *Sex Work*; see also McClintock, "Screwing the System"; Ross, *No Respect*; and Vance, *Pleasure and Danger*.

7. See Mohanty, Russo, and Torres, *Third World Women*; and Basu, "Sexual Imperialism."

8. Hebdige, *Subculture*; see pt. 2: A Reading, esp. "The Function of Subculture," 73–79, "Style in Revolt: Revolting Style," 100–102, and "From Culture to Hegemony," 5–19.

9. Haraway, "The Promises of Monsters." Also see Trinh Minh-ha, *Woman, Native, Other*.

10. For some discussions of the use of the term "queer," see Sedgwick, "Queer Performativity"; and Butler, "Critically Queer"; also Abelove, Barale, and Halperin, *The Lesbian and Gay Studies Reader*; and its critique by Butler, "Against Proper Objects."

11. See Rubin, "Thinking Sex" for a survey of some of these practices, the cultural responses to them, and an analysis of how a theory of benign sexual variation might produce an ethics of tolerance.

12. See Frecerro, "Notes of a Post–Sex Wars Theorizer."

13. Clifford, "Traveling Cultures."

14. hooks, "Feminism," 19–27.

15. Haraway, "The Promises of Monsters," 300.

16. For a detailed philosophical and literary discussion of the vampire as a figure for queer, see Case, "Tracking the Vampire."

17. Gomez, *The Gilda Stories*. The epigraph by Lorde is quoted from "Prologue" in Lorde, *From a Land Where Other People Live*.

18. See also Freccero, "Our Lady of MTV."

19. For a discussion of Madonna's crotch grabbing, see Garber, *Vested Interests*, 118–27.

20. For a discussion of this term, see Said, *Orientalism*.

21. See Cherríe Moraga's comment about the 1982 Barnard Conference's Speakout on Politically Incorrect Sex, which acknowledges the existence of erotically pleasurable redeployments of experiences of political violence and calls for their analysis in a context that would respect people's erotic rights: "What does it mean that some images and acts of s/m sex mirror actual acts of violence visited upon people of color, Jews, and women as a group—and that some Jewish women and women of color are sexually stimulated by these?" Freccero, "Notes of a Post–Sex Wars Theorizer," 312–13.

22. See Madonna's book *Sex*, where she makes a more explicit case for this reading of her cultural production involving sexuality.

23. See Jordan, "Black History as Myth," in *Civil Wars*, 163–68.

24. For feminist discussions of women in relation to popular musical genres, see in particular McRobbie, *Feminism and Youth Culture*; Lewis, *Gender Politics and MTV*; and Frith and McRobbie, "Rock and Sexuality."

25. See hooks, "Madonna: Plantation Mistress or Soul Sister?"

26. See Frith, "The Cultural Study of Popular Music," for an argument about the meaning of Black music for whites in popular music.

27. Freccero, "Our Lady of MTV," 181–82.

28. See Van Meter, "Madonna's Boyz Express Themselves to Jonathan Van Meter" (interview); see also Vickers, "Maternalism and the Material Girl"; and Shewey, "The Gospel according to Madonna" (interview). Much of this analysis owes a debt to conversations with, and the work of, Nancy Vickers.

29. See Holden, "Madonna Re-Creates Herself."

30. It is interesting in this context to consider the efforts Madonna has exercised to shield her social and biological act of mothering (to the child she bore) from public popular representation and comment.

31. I wish to thank Robert Miotke of the rhetoric department at the University of California, Berkeley, for drawing to my attention the fag hag dimension of Madonna's performance in *Truth or Dare*.

Notes to Chapter 4

1. Bhabha, "Postcolonial Authority"; Mercer, "'1968': Periodizing Postmodern Politics." For further discussions of racialization in the British cul-

tural studies context, see Baker, Diawara, and Lindeborg, *Black British Cultural Studies*; for a discussion of Black popular culture, see Dent, *Black Popular Culture*.

2. The quote is "the decolonizing of our minds," in hooks, *Yearning*, 5. See also hooks, "Representing Whiteness," 346.

3. For a theoretical discussion of how bodies come into being socially, see Butler, *Bodies That Matter*.

4. See Foucault's discussion of reverse discourse in *The History of Sexuality:*

> There is no question that the appearance in nineteenth-century psychiatry, jurisprudence, and literature of a whole series of discourses on the species and subspecies of homosexuality . . . made possible a strong advance of social controls into this area of "perversity"; but it also made possible the formation of a "reverse" discourse: homosexuality began to speak in its own behalf, to demand that its legitimacy or "naturality" be acknowledged, often in the same vocabulary, using the same categories by which it was medically disqualified. There is not, on the one side, a discourse of power, and opposite it, another discourse that runs counter to it. Discourses are tactical elements or blocks operating in the field of force relations; there can exist different and even contradictory discourses within the same strategy; they can, on the contrary, circulate without changing their form from one strategy to another, opposing strategy. (101–2)

5. Cisneros, *Woman Hollering Creek*; Chabram-Dernersesian, "I Throw Punches for My Race"; Anzaldúa, *Borderlands*; and Moraga, *Loving in the War Years*.

6. Jordan, "Waiting for a Taxi"; see also Freccero, "June Jordan"; the term "coalition politics" comes from Reagon, "Coalition Politics." For an articulation of how identity politics might work as a strategy rather than an ontology or epistemology, see Spivak, "In a Word. Interview," on "strategic essentialism."

7. hooks, "Is Paris Burning?"

8. See Trinh Minh-ha, "Not You/Like You."

9. See Butler, "Gender Is Burning," in *Bodies That Matter*, for another reading of the film's engagement with gender:

> Venus, and *Paris Is Burning* more generally, calls into question whether parodying the dominant norms is enough to displace them; indeed, whether the denaturalization of gender cannot be the very vehicle for a

reconsolidation of hegemonic norms. . . . At best, it seems, drag is a site of a certain ambivalence, one which reflects the more general situation of being implicated in the regimes of power by which one is constituted and, hence, of being implicated in the very regimes of power that one opposes. (125)

10. Mohanty, Russo, and Torres, preface to *Third World Women*, ix–x.

11. Mohanty, "Introduction: Cartographies of Struggle," 13–14.

12. Harlow, "The Theoretical-Historical Context," in *Resistance Literature*, 1–30.

13. See Said, *Culture and Imperialism*.

14. See Fanon, *The Wretched of the Earth*; for discussions of the relation between nationalisms and sexuality, see Parker et al., *Nationalisms and Sexualities*.

15. Mohanty, Russo, and Torres, *Third World Women*, 51–80.

16. See Derrida, *Positions*; also Culler, *On Deconstruction*, esp. "Writing and Logocentrism," 89–110:

In oppositions such as meaning/form, soul/body, intuition/expression, literal/metaphorical, nature/culture, intelligible/sensible, positive/negative, transcendental/empirical, serious/non-serious, the superior term belongs to the logos and is a higher presence; the inferior term marks a fall. Logocentrism thus assumes the priority of the first term and conceives the second in relation to it, as a complication, a negation, a manifestation, or a disruption of the first. (93)

17. See Laplanche, "Castrations et symbolisations," in which he explains the difference in Freud between *der Unterschied* (difference) and *Verschiedenheit* (diversity). I thank Barbara Spackman for drawing this text to my attention.

18. See Lacan, "The Signification of the Phallus"; see also Mitchell and Rose, *Feminine Sexuality*, "Introduction-I" and in particular, "Introduction-II," 47–54.

19. My reading of Butler's *Dawn* in the context of postcolonial theory is largely indebted to Cherniavsky, "Subaltern Studies in a U.S. Frame": "In the defamiliarized landscape of the science fiction text, Butler offers a polemical vision of U.S. slavery as an explicitly colonial practice, even as the novel moves forward to imagine the conditions for the emergence of both the colonizer and the colonized as postnational subjects" (104). On reproductive technologies and their imbrication with race in the United States, see Davis, "Outcast Mothers and Surrogates." For another reading of Butler, see Haraway, "The

Biopolitics of Postmodern Bodies," 225–30; and "A Cyborg Manifesto," 176–79.

20. See my discussion of utopia, Freccero, "Thélème: Temporality, Utopia, Supplement," in *Father Figures,* 104–28; also Jameson, "Magical Narratives."

Notes to Chapter 5

1. Chabram-Dernersesian, "I Throw Punches for My Race," 82.

2. On "riding on the hyphen," see Gerard, "David Hwang." Since this article was written, it has become common practice not to include a hyphen in the modification of "American"; thus I do not use it here.

3. Chabram-Dernersesian, "I Throw Punches for My Race," 81–82.

4. hooks, "Counter-Hegemonic Art"; see also Dent, *Black Popular Culture.*

5. For a discussion of *la Malinche*, see Moraga, *Loving in the War Years,* 99–100; and Anzaldúa, *Borderlands.*

6. See also Chabram-Dernersesian's discussion of revisioning *la Virgen*, 91.

7. One of the legends or myths is that *la Malinche* and *la Llorona* are one and the same person, and that she acquired the name *la Llorona* when Cortés returned to Spain, taking their son with him; thus *la Llorona* weeps for the loss of her son. Cisneros refers to *la Llorona* as "the one who drowned her own children" (51). For a delightfully queer rewriting of the myth of *la Llorona*, see Palacios, "La Llorona Loca."

8. Wallace, "Negative Images," 655–56. She refers to an essay by Saakana, "Mythology and History: An Afrocentric Perspective of the World": "In Saakana's account, European and British imperialism in the seventeenth and eighteenth centuries was inevitably accompanied by the development of 'history,' as a form of narrative discourse considered by the Enlightenment as infinitely superior to 'myth,' which then was made to stand in for all other approaches to the past" (655). The term "resistance narrative" is adapted here from Harlow, *Resistance Literature.* She defines resistance literature as literature that "calls attention to itself, and to literature in general, as a political and politicized activity. The literature of resistance sees itself furthermore as immediately and directly involved in a struggle against ascendant or dominant forms of ideological and cultural production" (28). "Whereas the social and the personal have tended to displace the political in western literary and cultural studies, the emphasis in the literature of resistance is on the political as the power to change the world. The theory of resistance literature is in its politics" (30).

9. See hooks, "Counter-Hegemonic Art"; and Wallace, "Spike Lee and Black Women," in *Invisibility Blues*, 100–106.

10. Kipnis, "(Male) Desire and (Female) Disgust."

11. What *Hustler* does in this regard is similar to the move Eldridge Cleaver made in *Soul on Ice* that so outraged feminists. In his confessional autobiography, Cleaver notes that, in order to "practice" his plan to rape white women to avenge himself, and Black men generally, against white male supremacy, he would rape Black women in his neighborhood. Thus Cleaver ironically underscores the error he committed through a displacement of class and racial antagonism that colluded with masculinist notions of women as property, and he demonstrates the political liabilities—as well as the damage and abuse—entailed by his mystification.

12. See Anna Deavere Smith's performance piece about the Los Angeles rebellion, *Twilight—Los Angeles 1992*, which highlights the issues at stake in what was perceived to be interracial conflict. She also does this in her piece about the Crown Heights, Brooklyn, incident in *Fires in the Mirror*.

13. The groups rendered invisible in this discourse about Los Angeles were Chicanos and Latinos, and we see that in Spike Lee's film the Puerto Ricans are aligned on the side of the African Americans in terms of their dispossession and their political allegiances.

14. See Lee with Jones, *Do the Right Thing: A Spike Lee Joint*.

15. hooks, *Yearning*, 176; and Wallace, *Invisibility Blues*, 108. The two quotations appear as text, in the following order (one above the other, so that the audience reads them "scrolling downward"):

> Violence as a way of achieving racial justice is both impractical and immoral. It is impractical because it is a descending spiral ending in destruction for all. The old law of an eye for an eye leaves everybody blind. It is immoral because it seeks to humiliate the opponent rather than win his understanding. It seeks to annihilate rather than to convert. Violence is immoral because it thrives on hatred rather than love. It destroys community and makes brotherhood impossible. It leaves society in monologue rather than dialogue. Violence ends by defeating itself. It creates bitterness in the survivors and brutality in the destroyers. Martin Luther King, Jr.

> I think there are plenty of good people in America, but there are also plenty of bad people in America, and the bad ones are the ones who seem to have all the power and be in these positions to block things that you and I need. Because this is the situation, you and I have to preserve the right to do what is necessary to bring an end to that situation, and it doesn't mean that I advocate violence, but at the same time I am not

against using violence in self-defense. I don't even call it violence when it's self-defense, I call it intelligence. Malcolm X.

16. In *Jungle Fever*, John Turturro is the Italian American who is not racist and who dates an African American woman at the end of the film; he gets beaten up in the process.

17. Gates, introduction to *Loose Canons*, xi–xix. On the 2 Live Crew controversy, see also Crenshaw, "Beyond Racism and Misogyny: Black Feminism and 2 Live Crew"; Gates, "2 Live Crew, Decoded"; and Santoro, "How 2 B Nasty." For a different point of view regarding the lyrics of "As Nasty as They Wanna Be," see Freccero, "Unruly Bodies."

18. Some examples include Paul Simon's transplanting of the South African singing group Ladysmith Black Mambazo; Sting's album *Nothing Like the Sun*, which combines Brazilian and other South American music with American rock and roll; and Peter Gabriel's "discovery" and use of the music of Nusrat Fateh Ali Khan for primarily "Western"-based melodies and lyrics.

19. Kobena Mercer also comments on the signification of "Blackness" and the differences between American and British uses of the term. See Mercer, "'1968': Periodizing Postmodern Politics"; also *Welcome to the Jungle*. For a discussion of Blackness and music in a comparative Anglo/U.S. context, see Gilroy, *The Black Atlantic*.

20. I use the term "homosocial" here, rather than "homoerotic," because gay sexuality is precisely what is covered over or silenced or denied in the myth of this youth subculture.

21. For a discussion of pop and the feminine and women artists in pop, see Lewis, *Gender Politics and MTV*; also McRobbie, *Feminism and Youth Culture*.

22. See Davis and Houston, *The Bodyguard*.

23. The soundtrack album is co-executively produced by Whitney Houston; all the new songs were written and produced by the young Black talent Babyface. See Edmonds, Houston, and Davis, *Waiting to Exhale*.

24. Babyface, "Not Gon' Cry," sung by Mary J. Blige (appearing courtesy of Uptown Records/MCA Records); see Edmonds, Houston, and Davis, *Waiting to Exhale*.

25. Tim Robbins writes a piece that is featured in the notes for the album. See Robbins and Robbins, *Dead Man Walking*.

Notes to Chapter 6

1. Bruno, "Ramble City," 63.
2. Bruno, "Ramble City":

Jameson suggests that the postmodern condition is characterized by a
schizophrenic temporality and a spatial pastiche . . . schizophrenia is ba-
sically a breakdown of the relationship between signifiers, linked to the
failure of access to the Symbolic. With pastiche there is an effacement of
key boundaries and separations, a process of erosion of distinctions. Pastiche is intended as an aesthetic of quotations pushed to the limit; it is
an incorporation of forms, an imitation of dead styles deprived of any
satirical impulse. (62)

3. See Jameson, "Postmodernism and Consumer Society": "The schizophrenic does not have our sense of temporal continuity but is condemned to
live a perpetual present with which the various moments of his or her past
have little connection and for which there is no conceivable future on the
horizon" (119). See also Jameson, "Postmodernism, or The Cultural Logic of
Late Capitalism"; Baudrillard, "The Ecstasy of Communication"; Deleuze
and Guattari, *Anti-Oedipus*.

4. Debord, *The Society of the Spectacle*.

5. See also Baudrillard, *Simulations*.

6. See, among others, Godzich, "Foreword: The Further Possibility of
Knowledge."

7. "It belonged, he knew—he remembered—as she pulled him down, to
the meat, the flesh the cowboys mocked. It was a vast thing, beyond knowing,
a sea of information coded in spiral and pheromone, infinite intricacy that
only the body, in its strong blind way, could ever read," *Neuromancer*, 239.

8. Sofia, "Exterminating Fetuses."

9. Fitting, "The Lessons of Cyberpunk"; Stone, "Will the Real Body Please
Stand Up?"

10. Ross, "Hacking Away at the Counterculture":

Studies of youth subcultures . . . have taught us that the political meaning of certain forms of cultural "resistance" is notoriously difficult to
read. . . . If cultural studies of this sort have proved anything, it is that
the often symbolic, not wholly articulate, expressivity of a youth culture
can seldom be translated directly into an articulate political philosophy.
The significance of these cultures lies in their embryonic or *protopolitical* languages and technologies of opposition to dominant or parent systems of rules. (122)

11. On homosociality, see Sedgwick, *Between Men*.

12. For another discussion of the potentially progressive aspects of a technocultural reconfiguration, see Haraway, "A Cyborg Manifesto."

13. See Frith, "The Cultural Study of Popular Music."

14. I treat the *Alien* films here as a trilogy because at the time, the fourth film had not yet appeared. At the same time, these three films mark themselves as a trilogy by the third film, which uses "to the third power" as a way of connecting itself to the other two. The fourth, *Alien: Resurrection*, announces itself as a belated arrival by the term "resurrection." Nevertheless, its thematics also engage current popular and public meditations on reproduction, technology (including reproductive technology and genetic engineering), and the question of the in/human and posthuman futures for the world.

15. Wood, "Return of the Repressed," 26. For issues involving generic hybridization, see Wood, "Cross Talk."

16. See Jameson, *The Political Unconscious*, 76, 115–18.

17. Anderson, "Monkey's Paw," from *Strange Angels*.

18. See Said, *Culture and Imperialism*:

> if it is true that Conrad ironically sees the imperialism of the San Tomé silver mine's British and American owners as doomed by its own pretentious and impossible ambitions, it is also true that he writes as a man whose Western view of the non-Western world is so ingrained as to blind him to other histories, other cultures, other aspirations. All Conrad can see is a world totally dominated by the Atlantic West, in which every opposition to the West only confirms the West's wicked power. (xviii–xix)

Since Conrad's *Nostromo* is located in Central America, it is perhaps no accident that the second film of the trilogy, *Aliens*, will pun incessantly on the question of illegal aliens through the marine Vasquez, her occasional exclamations in Spanish, and her locker room motto, *El riesgo siempre vive*. In *Alien*, *Nostromo* (our man/boatswain) is the cargo ship that ultimately and unwittingly becomes the dramatic vehicle where the battle of values between the female/feminist hero Ripley and the company/computer "MU TH UR" gets played out.

19. Ross, "New Age Technoculture," 531.

20. See Haraway, "The Promises of Monsters"; and Ross, "New Age Technoculture."

21. Virilio, "Aliens."

22. Curiously, *Aliens* recognizes the changed identity formations of the United States and explicitly addresses feminism. These features of the film, argues Christine Holmlund, are typical of what she calls the New Cold War sequels of the eighties, where

> economic fears become rewritten as sexual dilemmas, and white subcultures and racial minorities become subsumed within or behind the

white middle class family. Yet the presence of strong female, non-white and/or counter-cultural characters does indicate that social change has occurred and is occurring. Like a thread that runs throughout their fictions, . . . [these] films depict a resurgent United States' posture of strength, yet the films also refer constantly to fear of weakness. Memories about both Vietnam and social protest coexist and collide as cinematic fictions use the past and future to shore up, disguise or replace the present. ("*Down and Out in Beverly Hills, Rocky IV, Aliens*: New Cold War Sequels and Remakes," 86)

23. On recognition codes, see Lewis, *Gender Politics and MTV*; also Fiske, *Television Culture.*

24. In this connection, see Kipnis, "(Male) Desire and (Female) Disgust."

25. Kavanaugh, "'Son of a Bitch': Feminism, Humanism, and Science in *Alien*."

26. At the time of this writing, the fourth *Alien* film was being prepared. *Alien: Resurrection* featured Ripley as a genetic mutant.

27. See, in particular, Dargis, "*Alien³* and Its Metaphors"; and Taubin, "Invading Bodies," 9–10.

28. The YY can function as a gay encoding device; it resembles more the drawing of two male symbols together, ubiquitous graffiti signifier of gay love.

29. Taubin, "Invading Bodies": "AIDS is everywhere in the film. It's in the danger surrounding sex and drugs. It's in the metaphor of a mysterious deadly organism attacking an all-male community. It's in the iconography of shaven heads" (10).

30. I wish to thank Daniel Selden of UCSC for pointing out this aspect of the film to me, and for first suggesting to me that *Alien³* had progressive political potential.

31. Scobie, "What's the Story, Mother?"

32. Scobie is citing Abraham and Torok's works *The Wolfman's Magic Word* and *The Shell and the Kernel.*

33. Perhaps this is a sign of continued unease with the meaning of "race" in a country that sends to state-sanctioned death a disproportionate number of specifically Black murderers and rapists. Surely the film distances Dillon from his murderer/rapist identity in order to elicit a middle-class and predominantly white empathy for his heroic, if useless, death.

34. Suicide does, in fact, have a history of oppositional valorization: examples include the Buddhist monks in Vietnam, whose self-immolation spoke in eloquent protest of the war, and numerous recent deployments of the hunger

strike, where the consent to death is read as directly confrontational to the state. See also Malcomsin, "Socialism or Death?"

35. This recalls another sexy moment in the film, so sexy it serves as its advertising trailer: when the alien sidles up to Ripley after possessively killing off her sex partner, but does not touch her. We are puzzled then, but we later learn it is because she carries "its" child.

36. Bersani, *The Culture of Redemption*. I am thinking of Crimp, "How to Have Promiscuity in an Epidemic"; Bersani, "Is the Rectum a Grave?"; and Dean's remarkable article "The Psychoanalysis of AIDS," which all suggest a rejection of the culture of redemption and a theorization of the death drive as the (homosexual) *jouissance* of the Other.

37. Diamanda Galas, for example, promotes a T-shirt that reads, "We are all HIV+."

38. I also want to suggest that the use of nationalistic rhetoric for the queer cause, as in the Lesbian Avengers' motto, "Lesbian Avengers: We Recruit," and in the term "Queer Nation," though it is an example of what Foucault terms "counter-discourse," becomes problematic in its parodic intent when it converges with the current debate on gays in the military and with the "gay menace" response. For a discussion that problematizes queer nationalism, see Kalin, "Slant: Tom Kalin on Queer Nation."

GLOSSARY

*With Robin Baldridge
and Catherine Newman*

agency: The ability to act and its realization. Agency, as it is used here, suggests the continued possibility of action within the framework of constraint. "The question of agency constitutes another tension both within and around post-colonial theory. Post-structuralism in particular has criticised existing models of individual subjectivity, above all the bourgeois liberal concept of the autonomous individual" (Williams and Chrisman, *Colonial Discourse and Post-Colonial Theory*, 6).

articulate: To pronounce clearly and distinctly, to join together in sections, to utter distinctly. "Articulation" is often used to distinguish a particular kind of critique from notions such as "representation," "understanding" and "explanation," which presuppose a subject/object relation between the knower and what is known. Articulation may complicate rather than explain phenomena, in order to convey more accurately the complexity of such phenomena and our ability to understand them. "Articulation is not a simple matter. Language is the effect of articulation, and so are bodies. . . . Nature may be speechless, without language, in the human sense; but nature is highly articulate. Discourse is only one process of articulation" (Haraway, "The Promises of Monsters," 324). "The represented is reduced to the permanent status of the recipient of action, never to be a co-actor in an articulated practice among unlike, but joined, social partners" (Haraway, "The Promises of Monsters," 312; see 311–13 for the distinction she draws between articulation and representation).

| 149 |

bildungsroman: A German term meaning "formation novel," used to refer to novels that follow the development of the hero or heroine from childhood or adolescence into adulthood, through a troubled quest for identity.

binary opposition: The West's conceptual organization of the world in terms of mutually exclusive contrasting pairs, for example, light/dark, same/other, male/female. Deconstruction aims to expose the exclusions produced through these oppositions and to demonstrate that although one term is given positive meaning while the other is seen as derivative or negatively valorized, each term is absolutely dependent on the other for its meaning. "The simplest form of such oppositions, and at the same time the most profoundly dialectical, is a tension between presence and absence, between positive and negative (or zero) signs, in which one of the two terms of the binary opposition 'is apprehended as positively having a certain feature while the other is apprehended as deprived of the feature in question'" (Jameson, *The Prison-House of Language*, 35).

bourgeois: Most simply put, this French term refers to the middle class. "Associated with Marxist thought/critique—referring in Marx to established and solvent burgesses and a growing class of traders, entrepreneurs and employers, but additionally referring to bourgeois ideology; e.g., of the individual citizen, art, thought, manners. For Marx, different stages of bourgeois society led to different stages of the capitalist mode of production" (Williams, *Keywords*, 37–39).

capitalism: An economic system involving the ownership of the means of production by capitalists, who extract profit from workers through the wage labor system. Historically, capitalism is seen as having emerged from a developing bourgeois society in Europe in the sixteenth century; industrial capitalism reached its apex in the late eighteenth and early nineteenth centuries (see Williams, *Keywords*, 42–43).

colonialism: The conquest and control of other people's land. The term generally refers to the process whereby a metropolitan center establishes colonies in a noncapitalist region, replaces that region's government, social organization, and economic system with its own, and subjugates that region's people. The metropole aims to colonize a region in order to exploit its human and natural resources for economic profit. Historically, the great age of colonialism refers to the rapid acquisition of territories by European nations in the late nineteenth century. Williams and Chrisman argue that this moment "represent[ed] the need for access to new (preferably captive) markets and sources of raw materials, as well as the desire to deny these to competitor nations" (Williams and Chrisman, *Colonial Discourse and Post-Colonial Theory*, 2). "The term 'colonization' has been used to characterize everything from the most evident economic and political hierarchies to the production of a particular cultural discourse about what is called the 'Third World'. However sophisticated or problematical its use as an explanatory construct, colonization almost invariably implies a relation of structural domination, and a discursive or political suppression of the heterogeneity of the subject(s) in question" (Mohanty, "Under Western Eyes," 196). See also **imperialism**.

commodity culture: Postmodern culture in which commodities and "art" have become intimately associated, such that commodity production and consumption come to determine other aspects of culture. "What has happened is that aesthetic production today has become integrated into commodity production generally: the frantic economic urgency of producing fresh waves of ever more novel-seeming goods (from clothing to airplanes), at ever greater rates of turnover, now assigns an increasingly essential structural function and position to aesthetic innovation and experimentation. Such economic necessities then find recognition in the varied kinds of institutional support available for the newer art, from foundations and grants to museums and other forms of patronage" (Jameson, *Postmodernism*, 4–5).

crossover: Traditionally, a Black musical artist who makes it onto the white charts; recently white musical artists have aspired to the position of reverse crossover, making it onto the Black charts as well as the white ones.

cultural imperialism: Imperialism, which is closely related to expansionism, generally refers to the practice of a dominating metropolitan center, or empire, in relation to a distant territory. Colonialism, the setting up of settler colonies on that territory, is often a consequence of imperialism. Imperialism may be formal and systemic, involving military conquest, or it may be informal, involving the production of economic, political, social, and cultural dependence on the metropole in the territory. As Edward Said notes, "In our time, direct colonialism has largely ended; imperialism, as we shall see, lingers where it has always been, in a kind of general cultural sphere as well as in specific political, ideological, economic, and social practices" (Said, *Culture and Imperialism*, 9). For a discussion of the full complexities of this term, see Tomlinson, *Cultural Imperialism*.

cultural relativism: Often opposed to the concept of ethnocentrism, which is the perception of any and all cultures from the exclusive point of view of one's own. Also often opposed to universalism, a view whereby all humans and therefore all cultures share a certain set of moral values or certain other fundamental characteristics that could be said to constitute the nature of humanity. Cultural relativism thus can be seen to "stress the particularist nature and the relative character of the values promoted by different societies" (Amselle, *Logiques métisses*, 35). Verdier, in "Chercher remède à l'excision," offers an argument about the relative liabilities of cultural relativism and universalism: "pure cultural relativism . . . undermines the unity of the human race . . . totalitarian pseudo-universalism . . . would refuse the right to difference and lead to the negation of all cultural and religious identity" (149). For an interesting discussion of cultural relativism and universalism, especially in the context of feminist debates about female excision, see Lionnet, *Postcolonial Representations*.

cyberpunk: First associated with William Gibson's novel *Neuromancer* (1984), cyberpunk is a branch of SF that is derived from "hard science fiction" dating from the 1930s and the "new wave" of science fiction in the 1960s. It can be loosely characterized as representing "dark, pragmatic, and paranoid urbanism" (Bukatman, *Terminal Identity*, 141).

cyberspace: The term "cyberspace" comes from cyberpunk fiction: it is "a completely malleable realm of transitory data structures in which historical time is measured in nanoseconds and spatiality somehow exists both globally and invisibly" (Bukatman, *Terminal Identity*, 18).

cyborg: Term coined by Manfred Clynes and Nathan Kline in 1960, short for "cybernetic organism," now primarily associated with the work of Donna Haraway. Cyborg blurs the boundaries between human and machine or organism and machine; cyborg is an interface between organisms and machines. One can no longer understand human as an ontological status; "the human is presented as one part of a broader technological matrix" (Bukatman, *Terminal Identity*, 322).

deconstruction: Variously described as a method, a theory, or a philosophy, deconstruction, a term associated with the work of the French philosopher Jacques Derrida, involves the critique of logocentrism, Western philosophy's tendency to ascribe positive presence and a plenitude of meaning to one conceptual pole of a system of binary oppositions. Deconstruction has been most useful in the fields of philosophy and literary and linguistic theory, where it performs the work of demystification and resignification.

dialectical: A term made famous by Marx, following Hegel. In its most general sense, dialectical refers to the way contradictory forces interact. "In ancient Greece, dialectic was a form of reasoning that proceeded by question and answer, used by Plato. In later antiquity and the Middle Ages, the term was often used to mean simply logic, but Kant applied it to arguments showing that principles of science have contradictory aspects. Hegel thought that all logic and world history itself followed a dialectical path, in which internal contradictions were transcended, but gave rise to new contradictions that themselves required resolution. Marx and Engels gave Hegel's idea of dialectic a material basis; hence dialectical materialism" (Honderich, *The Oxford Companion to Philosophy*).

diasporic culture, diaspora: While diaspora originally refers to the scattering of the Jews described in the Hebrew Bible, the term has been taken up to refer to peoples and cultures that, as a result of the slave trade and colonization, have been geographically scattered throughout the world. Diasporic culture takes up what was initially a liability or a loss, and turns it into a distinctive and culturally affirming identity that can celebrate "homelessness" as well as mourn it. "A new structure of cultural exchange has been built up across the imperial networks which once played host to the triangular trade of sugar, slaves and capital. Instead of three nodal points there are now four—the Caribbean, the US, Europe, and Africa" (Gilroy, "*There Ain't No Black in the Union Jack*," 157). For Gilroy, "the dispersal or diaspora of black slave labourers should not be conceived of in exclusively economic terms; the diaspora also created a network of 'cultural sub-systems'" (158).

disavowal: According to Freud, the formula of fetishistic disavowal is "I know very well, but nonetheless . . ."; thus disavowal is both a recognition and a refusal of that recognition. "It is not true that the child emerges from his experience of seeing the female parts with an unchanged belief in the woman having a phallus. He retains this belief but he also gives it up; . . . a compromise is constructed" (Freud, "Fetishism," 216).

discourse: The term is most commonly associated with the work of Michel Foucault. Most generally, it refers to the way language is organized into ideologically meaningful domains in a given culture. One refers, for example, to specialized fields of knowledge as having their own discourses, as in the discourse of law, medicine, and so forth. The term "refers to socially produced groups of ideas or ways of thinking that can be tracked in individual texts or groups of texts, but that also demand to be located within wider historical and social structures or relations" (Turner, *British Cultural Studies*, 32–33).

dominant culture: The culture in a given society that imposes itself on all members of that society as the norm or the preferred culture. Stuart Hall remarks, "Any society's culture tends, with varying degrees of closure, to impose its classification of the social and cultural and political world. These constitute a *dominant cultural order*, though it is neither univocal nor uncontested" (quoted in Turner, *British Cultural Studies*, 91).

drag queen: A man—usually a gay man—who dresses up as a woman, for fun, for work, or for performances. He may also dress this way in everyday life.

enlightenment: A philosophical movement in the seventeenth and eighteenth centuries in Europe. Its assertions include a belief in the superior capacities of reason to enable humankind to think and act correctly. Humankind is thought to be, at base, rational and good, capable of perfectability. Enlightenment thinking is generally seen to come to an end with the fact of the Holocaust as the sign of humankind's ability to harness rationality for evil.

ethnocentrism: see **cultural relativism**.

ethnography: The description of the races of mankind. "The myth of the Lone Ethnographer thus depicts the birth of ethnography, a genre of social description. Drawing on models from natural history, such accounts usually moved upward from environment and subsistence through family and kinship to religion and spiritual life. Produced by and for specialists, ethnographies aspired to the holistic representation of other cultures; they portrayed other forms of life as totalities. Ethnographies were storehouses of purportedly incontrovertible information to be mined by armchair theorists engaged in comparative studies. This genre seemingly resembled a mirror that reflected other cultures as they 'really' were" (Rosaldo, *Culture and Truth*, 31–32).

fag hag: A woman, straight or gay, who hangs out with gay men, usually drag queens; a woman whose primary friends are gay men. The term is used affectionately within the community, although it can also be used in a derogatory manner.

fetishism: From the term "fetish," used to refer to an object that possesses extraordinary powers and is also often an object of worship. Two different but potentially interrelated senses of fetishism are derived from Marx and Freud. For Marx, commodity fetishism is "a definite social relation between men, that assumes, in their eyes, the fantastic form of a relation between things." Commodity fetishism "consists of a certain misrecognition which concerns the relation between a structured network of relations between elements, appears as an immediate property of one of the elements, as if this property also belongs to it outside its relation with other elements" (Žižek, *The Sublime Object of Ideology*, 23–24). For Freud, "the fetish is a penis-substitute . . . it is not a substitute for any chance penis, but for a particular quite special penis that had been extremely important in early childhood but was afterwards lost. That is to say: it should normally have been given up, but the purpose of the fetish precisely is to preserve it from being lost. To put it plainly: the fetish is a substitute for the woman's (mother's) phallus which the little boy once believed in and does not wish to forgo" (Freud, "Fetishism," 214–15).

film noir: "Dark film," a term applied by French critics to a type of American film, usually in the detective or thriller genres, with low-key lighting and a somber mood (Bordwell and Thompson, *Film Art,* 494).

genealogy: A constructional model of history, first identified by Nietzsche, that revises a linear model of history as evolutionary progression. Genealogy begins from the present and attempts to articulate the history of the particular ideology or ideologies that give rise to that present system. "In genealogical construction, we begin with a full blown system in terms of which elements of the past can 'artificially' be isolated as objective preconditions: genealogy is not a historical narrative, but has the essential function of renewing our perception of the synchronic system as in an x-ray, its diachronic perspectives serving to make perceptible the articulation of the functional elements of a given system in the present" (Jameson, *The Political Unconscious,* 139).

hegemony: A term associated with the Italian Marxist thinker Antonio Gramsci and frequently used in cultural studies. Gramsci's theory of hegemony holds that cultural domination is achieved through the consent of those whom it aims to subordinate. Furthermore, hegemony is conceived of as a dynamic process rather than a fixed condition. Thus certain oppositional beliefs in a culture, when they achieve a sufficiently widespread status as truths, can be thought to constitute counterhegemonies. In this way, the exercise of power by dominant social forces is seen to be subject to negotiation and change, rather than fixed and immutable.

heterosexism: The tendency of heterosexual culture to consider heterosexuality innately superior to homosexuality and the social system that arises from it. Most commonly, the term refers to the tendency of heterosexuals to forget or ignore the concerns and conditions of those who are not normatively heterosexual, such as gays and lesbians. Heterosexism describes the attitude that heterosexuality is the only sexuality that is natural and right; in practice, it can involve both ignoring and persecuting queers. While "homophobia" describes a hatred of homosexuality or homosexuals that is based on fear, "heterosexism" is, Sedgwick writes, "more suggestive of collective, structurally inscribed, perhaps materially based presumption" (Sedgwick, *Between Men*, 219 n. 1).

homosociality: Describes, most broadly, "social bonds between persons of the same sex" (Sedgwick, *Between Men*, 3). In more political terms, Sedgwick uses "homosociality" to describe the way patriarchal relations are structured as a triangle in which men negotiate power through women, who mediate but do not partake of this power. "Homosocial" is "a neologism, obviously formed by analogy with 'homosexual,' and just as obviously meant to be distinguished from 'homosexual.' In fact, it is applied to such activities as 'male bonding,' which may, as in our society, be characterized by intense homophobia, fear and hatred of homosexuality" (3). (See also Rubin, "The Traffic in Women.")

house cultures: Organizations of gay men, drag queens, transvestites, and transsexuals into "houses" named as such for the fashion industry, which is also organized by houses. Houses sponsor balls, which are fashion and dance competitions, and provide mutual support and assistance to their members, who are called children. Houses also have "mothers" and "fathers." (See *Paris Is Burning*; also Vickers, "Maternalism and the Material Girl.")

humanism: Originally a philosophy associated with the European Renaissance that placed humankind, rather than God, at the center of the universe. In modernity, humanism is more of an ideology and involves the belief in the centrality and superiority of humans in relation to the living world. Humanism has been criticized for concealing within its generality a very specific model of the human (usually male, usually white) and for elevating humans above the rest of the ecological system on which they are crucially dependent for life. "The Cartesian cogito 'I think therefore I am' exemplifies humanist ideology; the individual subject acts on the external world" (Honderich, *The Oxford Companion to Philosophy*).

hybridity: Most simply, a mixed-ness; used in postcolonial theory to refer to diasporic and postcolonial cultures and peoples. "Hybridity is the sign of the productivity of colonial power, its shifting forces and fixities; it is the name for the strategic reversal of the process of domination through disavowal (that is, the production of discriminatory identities that secure the 'pure' and original identity of authority)" (Bhabha, "Signs Taken for Wonders," 34–35).

identity politics: Struggles to oppose cultural domination on the basis of constructed identities, which take as their model in the United States the civil rights movements of the 1950s and 1960s, as well as the Black Power movement and Black nationalism. Identity politics, as struggles to resist racism, homophobia, and sexism, take up what is initially an identity imposed on people as one of the forms of domination. In other words, it is the dominators who first confer an identity on the dominated, in political terms, and that identity is a negative one: Black, gay, woman, and so on are initially defined in negative terms by the dominators. The people designated by these terms appropriate them for their own uses and definitions, invert the binary, reclaim the identity, and polemically define the identities in positive terms, using those originally negative identities as the basis for reclaiming rights as equals in the polity. Foucault terms this procedure "reverse discourse" (*The History of Sexuality*, vol. 1, 101).

ideologeme: The smallest identifiable component of an ideology, often used in the ideological critique of texts. Based on the term "seme," which is used in structuralist linguistic theory to refer to the smallest identifiable unit of meaning in language. An ideologeme is "the smallest intelligible unit of the essentially antagonistic collective discourses of social classes" (Jameson, *The Political Unconscious*, 76); also "a historically determined conceptual or semic complex which can project itself variously in the form of a 'value system,' or 'philosophical concept,' or in the form of a protonarrative, a private or collective narrative fantasy" (115).

ideology: The way a society explains itself to itself; a certain way of presenting the world that passes itself off as the truth of the world, that seems so self-evident that we take it as the truth. The term "ideology" has a long and complex history, from Marx through Althusser, whose definition is the one taken up within cultural studies. According to Marx, ideology is "a set of ideas which arise from a given set of material interests or from a definite class or group; also, abstract or false thought, illusion" (Williams, *Key-words*, 128–29).

imaginary: A structuring misrecognition between self and other that the French psychoanalyst Jacques Lacan refers to as the "mirror stage," where the infant sees itself reflected in the mirror in ideal-ized form. The child then takes up the reflection as a self-image. This initial moment of the formation of the subject (which will be completed by the oedipal complex [Freud] or the Symbolic stage [Lacan]) in part structures, visually and cognitively, a person's rela-tions to him/herself and with others, relations that are then subject to the distortions characteristic of mirror images. The Imaginary is thus the psychic structure originating from this developmental mo-ment. "In the sense given to this term by Jacques Lacan (and gen-erally used substantively): one of the three essential orders of the psychoanalytic field, namely the Real, the Symbolic and the Imagi-nary. The Imaginary order is characterized by the prevalence of the relation to the image of the counterpart; in Lacan's mirror stage, the ego of the infant is constituted on the basis of the image of the counterpart (e.g., the infant's reflection of itself in a mirror)" (La-planche and Pontalis, *The Language of Psychoanalysis*, 210).

imperialism: Related to the word empire/*imperium*: the policy by which a nation-state aspires to acquire additional territory and annex it to its own, thus expanding beyond its existing boundaries. This can take place on different levels and usually involves territorial annexation, economic and political annexation, juridical (legal) an-nexation, and ultimately ideological and cultural annexation; these latter come to be referred to as cultural imperialism. The term "cul-tural imperialism" can also be used to describe an attitude. See also **cultural imperialism**.

incorporation: A psychoanalytic term that Freud uses to talk about the difference between mourning and melancholia. Incorporation involves the fantasy of taking an object into the subject's body and preserving it there. It is originally a phenomenon associated with the oral stage in a child and is connected to the mouth and the in-gestion of food; on the psychic level, however, it has more general erotogenic implications and metaphorical effects. "Incorporation provides the corporal model for introjection and identification"

(Laplanche and Pontalis, *The Language of Psychoanalysis,* 211). According to Freud, incorporation is the psychic phenomenon that occurs in melancholia, whereby "the ego wishes to incorporate this object into itself, and the method by which it would do so, in this oral or cannibalistic stage, is by devouring it" ("Mourning and Melancholia," 171).

interpellation: A concept developed by the French Marxist philosopher Louis Althusser, interpellation refers to the way each of us is hailed by our social order in a particular way—how a social formation constructs and locates us as subjects who respond and consent to it in certain ways. "The subject is constructed in language and in discourse and, since the symbolic order in its discursive use is closely related to ideology, in ideology. It is in this sense that ideology has the effect, as Althusser argues, of constituting individuals as subjects, and it is also in this sense that their subjectivity appears 'obvious'. Ideology suppresses the role of language in the construction of the subject. As a result, people 'recognize' (misrecognize) themselves in the ways in which ideology 'interpellates' them, or in other words, addresses them as subjects, calls them by their names and in turn 'recognizes' their autonomy" (Belsey, *Critical Practice,* 61).

introjection: A psychoanalytic term related and opposed to incorporation. In introjection, the subject transposes the qualities of external objects to the inside of him/herself, thus integrating—and acknowledging as lost—the lost object with the self. "Introjection is close in meaning to incorporation, which indeed provides it with its bodily model, but it does not necessarily imply any reference to the body's real boundaries (introjection into the ego, into the ego-ideal, etc.). It is closely akin to identification" (Laplanche and Pontalis, *The Language of Psychoanalysis,* 229). Freud distinguishes introjection, which is what is supposed to occur in mourning, from incorporation, which is what occurs in melancholia. "The testing of reality, having shown that the loved object no longer exists, requires forthwith that all the libido shall be withdrawn from its attachments to this object. Against his demand a struggle of course arises—it may be universally observed that man never willingly abandons a libido-position, not even when a substitute is already

beckoning to him. . . . The normal outcome is that deference for reality gains the day" ("Mourning and Melancholia," 165–66).

***jouissance*:** The French word for "enjoyment" (often used to refer to
sexual orgasm). "[A term] employed by the critic Roland Barthes in
his *Le Plaisir du Texte* (1973) to suggest a kind of response to literary works that is different from ordinary *plaisir* (pleasure). Whereas
plaisir is comfortable and reassuring, confirming our values and expectations, jouissance—usually translated as 'bliss' to retain its
erotic sense—is unsettling and destabilizing" (Baldick, *The Concise
Oxford Dictionary of Literary Terms*).

logocentrism, logocentric: A term used by Derrida to refer to the
Western philosophical belief in the immediacy and self-present authenticity of speech as the expression of ideas in the mind as opposed to writing, which is seen as derivative, supplemental, secondary. Derrida demonstrates the extent to which this notion of the
immediacy and self-presence of speech in fact depends on writing
for its constitutive metaphor. (See also Honderich, *The Oxford
Companion to Philosophy*).

materialism: Materialism, as a philosophical concept, has a long and
complex history of multiple meanings. Reduced to its simplest relevant terms, modern philosophical materialism argues for the physical origin and causality of nature and human life (as against theological or spiritual explanations) and, in a corollary argument, for a
corresponding mechanical description of human life, moral behavior, and social organization. Karl Marx accepted the first premise,
but rejected the corollary in favor of a historical materialism that
recognized human agency and considered it a primary force.
Friedrich Engels generalized Marx's notion of the human activity of
production and its determinative nature into dialectical materialism
(the laws of historical development and of all natural and physical
processes).

mestizaje, mestiza/o: Chicano/a cultural identity that comes to embody the "new" notion of hybrid cultural identity, or *mestizaje—
mestiza/o* meaning mixed. A cultural identity thus founded not on a
notion of purity of heritage or origins, not on a notion of clearly
defined borders, but on a notion of loosely cohesive U.S./Mexi-
can/Latin American/indigenous American cultures whose hybrid-

ity or mixed-ness produces a kind of patchwork out of which the various strands cannot be separated. It celebrates *una raza mestiza*: "At the confluence of two or more genetic streams, with chromosomes constantly 'crossing over', this mixture of races, rather than resulting in an inferior being, provides hybrid progeny, a mutable, more malleable species with a rich gene pool. From this racial ideological, cultural and biological cross-pollenization, an 'alien' consciousness is presently in the making—a new *mestiza* consciousness, *una conciencia de mujer*. It is a consciousness of the Borderlands" (Anzaldúa, *Borderlands*, 77).

mise-en-abîme: The moment in a text where the theme or form of the text as a whole is reproduced or reduplicated in miniature within the text itself; akin to *Hamlet*'s play within a play.

narcissism: A concept used in psychoanalysis that also has common currency as a term in ordinary speech; love directed toward the image of oneself. From the myth, in Ovid's *Metamorphoses*, of Echo and Narcissus. "Freud speaks of primary narcissism, original in all humans ('an allocation of the libido such as deserved to be described as narcissism might be present far more extensively, and . . . might claim a place in the regular course of human sexual development'), and a secondary narcissism, acquired during development ('the narcissism which arises through the drawing in of object-cathexes'). The latter is what constitutes the narcissistic or ego-libido and, if not predominant over object-cathexes, determines a narcissistic object-choice—as, Freud suggests, in 'perverts and homosexuals'. If, however, it is predominant—as in 'narcissistic women,' whose need does not 'lie in the direction of loving, but of being loved' and who love only themselves 'with an intensity comparable to that of the man's love for them'—then the narcissistic or ego-libido stands in the way of a 'complete object-love' or 'is unfavorable to the development of a true object-love'" (De Lauretis, *The Practice of Love*, 188).

oedipal, Oedipus complex: A term coined by Freud to refer to a moment in the psychic development of the child when s/he must choose which parent with which to identify and which to desire. This involves, in traditional Freudian accounts, the young boy's rivalry with his father for the love of his mother, which resolves itself through the castration complex (the boy feels himself threatened with castration if he incurs the father's hostility) as identification with the father and desire for a woman who will substitute for the mother as the object of the boy's love. From the Greek play by Sophocles, *Oedipus Rex,* that tells the story of a man who kills his father and marries his mother. "Organised body of loving and hostile wishes which the child experiences towards its parents. In its so-called *positive* form, the complex appears as in the story of *Oedipus Rex*: a desire for the death of the rival—the parent of the same sex. In its *negative* form, we find the reverse picture: love for the parent of the same sex, and jealous hatred for the parent of the opposite sex. In fact, the two versions are to be found in varying degrees in what is known as the *complete* form of the complex" (Laplanche and Pontalis, *The Language of Psychoanalysis,* 282–83).

orientalism: A term made famous in modern times by Edward Said, used to refer to the particular construction of the East by the West, a construction that is a result of Western historical attempts to dominate the East and Western fantasies about the East as complement and opposite of the West, most prominent in Europe in the nineteenth century. "Orientalism is a style of thought based upon an ontological and epistemolgical distinction made between 'the Orient' and (most of the time) 'the Occident.' . . . Orientalism can be discussed and analyzed as the corporate institution for dealing with the Orient—dealing with it by making statements about it, authorizing views of it, describing it, by teaching it, settling it, ruling over it: in short, Orientalism as a Western style for dominating, restructuring, and having authority over the Orient" (Said, *Orientalism,* 2–3).

other: According to Lacan, we project negative feelings or fears from within ourselves onto other images or other people, creating a view of another person or group of people as being totally opposite to ourselves. "Lacan proposed the Symbolic pair of Subject and Other, which he defined in 1955 as 'the place where is constituted the I who speaks with the one who hears.' . . . Absolute pole of the address, but also Witness of the Truth, the Other is not a real interlocutor: it is essentially the Symbolic place required by speech of the subject, where the subject both *is,* and at the same time *is not,* in so far as he is constituted by lack in the Other" (Wright, *Feminism and Psychoanalysis*, 297–98).

patriarchy: Literally means the rule of the fathers: "the concept 'patriarchy' was re-discovered by the new feminist movement as a struggle concept, because the movement needed a term by which the totality of oppressive and exploitative relations which affect women, could be expressed as well as their systemic character. Moreover, the term 'patriarchy' denotes the historical and societal dimension of women's exploitation and oppression, and is thus less open to biologistic interpretations, in contrast, for example, to the concept of 'male dominance'" (Mies, *Patriarchy and Accumulation on a World Scale*, 37).

perversion: "For Freud, Deviation from the 'normal' sexual act when this is defined as coitus with a person of the opposite sex directed towards the achievement of orgasm by means of genital penetration; connotes the whole of the psychosexual behavior that accompanies such atypical means of obtaining sexual pleasure" (Laplanche and Pontalis, *The Language of Psychoanalysis*, 306).

phallus, phallic: The phallus, a term used by Lacan, refers generally to the symbolic power that accrues to the Father, or to men in patriarchal society. The phallus, as Lacan uses it, can wield this symbolic power only if it is veiled, that is, if its lack (the fact that it does not correspond to any particular positive power) is concealed or mystified, as it were. Although for Lacan the phallus is an arbitrary signifier, some critics have pointed out that there is a less than arbitrary relationship between the phallus as the chosen signifier and the penis, which was a key symbolic element for Freud. "The phallic signifier is, so to speak, an index of its own impossibility. In its very positivity it is the signifier of 'castration'—that is, of its own lack. The so-called pre-phallic objects (breasts, excrement) are lost objects, while the phallus is not simply lost but is an object which *gives body to a certain fundamental loss in its very presence. In the phallus, loss as such attains a positive existence*" (Žižek, *The Sublime Object of Ideology*, 156–57).

political correctness: Most often used by political conservatives to designate and deride a version of liberalism thought to be especially prevalent on college campuses, involving the efforts not to "offend" anyone, particularly members of minority groups, gays and lesbians, and the handicapped. Sometimes used by the Left to designate a superficial liberalism that seeks not to offend but does not seek social justice.

polysemic: Meaning different things to different people; refers to the multidimensional aspect of linguistic meaning. (See also Turner, *British Cultural Studies,* 36).

postcolonial: Relating to a body of theory that deals with the subjects and agents of decolonization in what is called the Third World. Sometimes it is used as a historical reference to the period after a war of decolonization, or the period after the great age of European colonialism, to indicate that colonialism has been superseded. Some object to this use of the term for the way it seems to gloss over the fact that many countries suffer from various forms of neocolonial domination. "Like any other form of 'post-', the post-colonial carries with it at least a dual sense of being chronologically subsequent to the second term in the relationship and of—on the face of it—having somehow superseded that term. The first of these is reasonably uncontentious: the era of formal colonial control is over, apart from aberrations such as the Falkland/Malvinas. If temporal succession is not a particular problem, however, supersession may still be" (Williams and Chrisman, *Colonial Discourse and Post-Colonial Theory,* 3–4).

postindustrial: Relating to the turn away from industrial optimism and visions of infinite prosperity through production to the industrial decay of late capitalist urban centers. "[A]s Daniel Bell and other theoreticians of the concept of a properly 'postindustrial society' have argued, it is now science, knowledge, technological research, rather than industrial production and the extraction of surplus value, that is the 'ultimately determining instance'" (Lyotard, *The Postmodern Condition,* xiii).

postmodernism: Various definitions of postmodernism exist; it can be thought of either as an aesthetic or as a historical period. Jameson's historical conception of postmodernism characterizes it "as the cultural dominant of the logic of late capitalism" (*Postmodernism,* 46). In postmodernism, "reification penetrates the sign itself and disjoins the signifier from the signified. Now reference and reality disappear altogether, and even meaning—the signified—is problematized. We are left with that pure and random play of signifiers that we call postmodernism, which no longer produces monumental works of the modernist type but ceaselessly reshuffles the fragments of preexistent texts, the building blocks of older cultural and social production, in some new and heightened bricolage" (96). "Notoriously vague in its definition, the key aspects of postmodernism . . . are its postulation of the disconnection between the signified and the signifier; the free play of the signifier privileging the power of the reader to decode the message in his or her own interests; and its celebration of the popular" (Turner, *British Cultural Studies*, 222).

power-knowledge: A term associated with Michel Foucault, referring to the way power is never separable from knowledge, and that truth always appears as a regime, that is, as truth that is produced rather than existing self-evidently on its own, outside power. "Foucault's notion of power/knowledge challenges assumptions that ideology can be demystified and, hence, that undistorted truth can be attained. . . . In rejecting the idea that power functions only through 'Thou shalt nots' or forms of restrictive commandments and laws, Foucault brings to our attention the complex network of disciplinary systems and prescriptive technologies through which power operated in the modern era, particularly since the normalizing disciplines of medicine, education, and psychology have gained ascendancy" (Diamond and Quinby, *Feminism and Foucault,* x–xi).

protopolitical: From Andrew Ross, "Hacking Away at the Counterculture": "Studies of youth subcultures . . . have taught us that the political meaning of certain forms of cultural 'resistance' is notoriously difficult to read. . . . If cultural studies of this sort have proved anything, it is that the often symbolic, not wholly articulate, expressivity of a youth culture can seldom be translated directly into an articulate political philosophy. The significance of these cultures lies in their embryonic or protopolitical languages and technologies of opposition to dominant or parent systems of rules" (122).

psychoanalysis: The founding of the discipline and practice of psychoanalysis can be attributed to Sigmund Freud (1856–1939), who began publishing papers on the unconscious in the early 1880s.

Psychoanalysis radically altered the notion of what constitutes a subject by introducing and theorizing the internal workings of the psyche vis-à-vis the subject's experience in the world. Since Freud, psychoanalysis has continued to develop not only as clinical practice (e.g., the talking cure), but also as cultural theory and as an influential dimension of literary criticism.

queer: Originally a derogatory term used to describe gays and lesbians. "Queer" is still a contested term among the gays and lesbians who originally took it up as a term of self-designation; it seems to have been an attempt to take a distance from the orthodoxies of a politically correct gay and lesbian culture that had a seemingly coherent definitional strategy (men who love men, women who love women) and politics. It emerged most forcefully around the new militancy centered on AIDS activism and groups such as ACT UP and Queer Nation, a militancy that refused the dominant culture's requirements that homosexuals somehow give up their "radical sex practices" or be damned. The term "queer" in some sense came into being to describe the disparate "inappropriate/d others" (Haraway's term) whose sexual practices and proclivities could not be made to fit the identity categories of either gay or straight, although, as many have pointed out, gay/lesbian sexual orientations continue to constitute the paradigmatic center for this non-identity category.

race: Race, in recent discussions of the term, has come to be thought of as a political category, the meaning accorded to human phenotypic variation. According to Paul Gilroy, "'Race' has to be socially and politically constructed and elaborate ideological work is done to secure and maintain the different forms of 'racialization' which have characterized capitalist development" (*"There Ain't No Black in the Union Jack,"* 38). Racialization or race formation refers to the way phenotypic variation has been transformed into elaborate systems of differentiation among groups of people based on race and color. It frequently involves appeals to biological theory for evidence.

radical sex practices: Refers most commonly to sexual practices regarded as non-normative within either straight or gay/lesbian sexual communities: for example, S/M, fisting, piercing, role playing, man/boy love. (See Rubin, "Thinking Sex," for a list of some of these.)

repression: A psychoanalytic term to describe the process whereby the subject attempts to repel or to confine to the unconscious particular thoughts, feelings, or memories, because they are seen to put the subject at risk. "Repression is particularly manifest in hysteria, but it also plays a major part in other mental illnesses as well as in normal psychology. It may be looked upon as a universal mental process insofar as it lies at the root of the constitution of the unconscious as a domain separate from the rest of the psyche. . . . In a looser sense, the term 'repression' is sometimes used by Freud in a way which approximates it to 'defence'" (Laplanche and Pontalis, *The Language of Psychoanalysis*, 390).

return of the repressed: The process by which that which has been repressed returns in distorted, displaced, or disguised form.

role playing: Notoriously difficult to define and characterize, and very contested, role playing often refers to the terms butch/femme, used to describe gay/lesbian partners who assume relatively gender-polarized roles.

semiotics: The study of linguistic and nonlinguistic signs and the production of meaning through sign-systems. Originally a term used in medicine for detecting illness on the basis of bodily signs. Semiotics as a field is attributed to both the American philosopher C. S. Peirce and the Swiss linguist Ferdinand de Saussure, founder of structuralist linguistics. See also **sign**.

sex/gender: The sex/gender system was most famously invoked in feminism by Gayle Rubin in "The Traffic in Women," to refer to social orders whereby distinct ideological meanings and roles are culturally assigned to persons on the basis of their biological sex. In this sense, then, "sex" refers to biological sex and "gender" refers to the social meaning accorded to it in a given society. However, more recently, Judith Butler has pointed out that the notion of biological sex already encodes within it the social meanings of gender. "Originally intended to dispute the biology-is-destiny formulation, the distinction between sex and gender serves the argument that whatever biological intractability sex appears to have, gender is culturally constructed: hence, gender is neither the causal result of sex nor as seemingly fixed as sex" (Butler, *Gender Trouble*, 6). However, "Gender ought not to be conceived merely as the cultural inscription of meaning on a pregiven sex (a juridical conception); gender must also designate the very apparatus of production whereby the sexes themselves are established. As a result, gender is not to culture as sex is to nature; gender is also the discursive/cultural means by which 'sexed nature' or 'a natural sex' is produced and established as 'prediscursive,' prior to culture, a politically neutral surface *on which* culture acts" (7).

sexuality: Commonly refers to sexual identity and sexual practices. Foucault argues that sexuality is a modern discourse that produces and deploys knowledge about sex as "the truth" of bodies and pleasures. Sex in turn becomes "the truth" of the individual. "The essential point is that sex was not only a matter of sensation and pleasure, of law and taboo, but also of truth and falsehood, that the truth of sex became something fundamental, useful, or dangerous, precious or formidable: in short, that sex was constituted as a problem of truth" (Foucault, *The History of Sexuality*, 56).

sign: The basic unit of meaning in language as in other sign-systems, or anything that has meaning. According to Saussure, a sign is composed of a signifier (the sensual and material aspect of the sign, such as a word or sound) and a signified (the conceptual meaning accorded the signifier). "In a linguistic sign, according to Saussure, the relationship between signifier and signified is 'unmotivated' or arbitrary; that is, it is based purely on social convention rather than on natural necessity: there is nothing about a horse which demands that it be called 'horse', since the French call the same thing *un cheval*. Saussure's theory deliberately leaves out the referent or real external object referred to by a sign. The alternative theory of the American philosopher C. S. Peirce has more room for referents and for 'motivated' signs. Peirce calls the unmotivated sign a symbol, while identifying two further kinds of sign: the icon, which resembles its referent (e.g., a photograph), and the index, which is caused by its referent (e.g., a medical symptom)" (Baldick, *The Concise Oxford Dictionary of Literary Terms*).

simulacrum: The copy that has no real as its referent, no real as that from which it originated; a simulation. (See, among others, Baudrillard, *Simulations*).

S/M: Sadomasochism, a radical sex practice involving the consensual use or exchange of force between persons. S/M has been the object of public controversy because of its often violent content and/or form. The term combines two distinct terms, sadism and masochism, each of which has its own literary and clinical history. Sadism is a term adapted from the name of the Marquis de Sade, who couched his political and philosophical allegories in representations of violent sexual encounters. Masochism comes from Sacher-Masoch, author of *Venus in Furs*, a novel about a man who enjoys submitting sexually to a dominating woman. Psychoanalysis takes up both of these terms to describe aspects of normative sexuality as well as to name specific sexual disorders.

subculture: A cultural formation within the dominant culture that can be distinguished by a stance, a style, an attitude, a position, a fashion as defiant, resistant, or oppositional to what is viewed as the dominant culture. Originally a term used in Britain to refer to youth cultures. Dick Hebdige describes subcultures as groups within the dominant or hegemonic culture that express a relation of resistance, opposition, or refusal to the larger culture or the hegemonic culture, that is, the culture that expresses the ruling order of any given social formation. Subcultures might be directly oppositional but usually are not—they challenge the hegemony indirectly or obliquely, through style: "The objections are lodged, the contradictions displayed, at the profoundly superficial level of appearances: that is, at the level of signs" (Hebdige, *Subculture*, 17).

technoculture: The culture that arises from and to a certain extent embraces the new technologies, perhaps most obviously illustrated by recent science fiction genres such as cyberpunk. "[T]he kinds of liberatory fantasies that surround new technologies are a powerful and persuasive means of social agency, . . . their source to some extent lies in real popular needs and desires. Technoculture, as we conceive it, is located as much in the work of everyday fantasies and actions as at the level of corporate or military decision making" (Penley and Ross, *Technoculture*, xiii).

transsexual: A person who identifies with the opposite sex, and who may alter his or her body to conform to this inner sense of gender identity. Transsexualism is to be distinguished from transvestitism, in which a person's pleasure, erotic or otherwise, may come from the dissonance between body and clothing.

trope: Originally from the Greek word *tropos*, meaning "to turn." Trope is the technical term in rhetoric for figure of speech.

uncanny: Freud discusses the uncanny in the context of literary effects; the word leads him to conduct a survey of the relation between *heimlich* and *unheimlich* (literally, "homely" or "familiar" and "un-homely"): "the uncanny is in reality nothing new or foreign, but something familiar and old-established in the mind that has been estranged only by the process of repression" ("The Uncanny," 148).

universalism: see **cultural relativism**.

voyeurism, voyeuristic: Most commonly used to describe the erotic pleasure of watching (often something forbidden) in secret. Voyeurism is commonly associated with the masculine position, while exhibitionism, its opposite and twin, is associated with femininity. Thus Freud considers voyeurism and exhibitionism the active and passive aspects of scopophilia, the drive to look. Much of feminist film theory has relied on Freud's notion of scopophilia to analyze the effects of film on spectators. "Laura Mulvey's landmark article 'Visual pleasure and narrative cinema' (1975) identified the position of the female filmic protagonist as exhibitionist object of the male gaze, and argued that, whether the audience was male or female, their spectatorial roles remain voyeuristic and function in complicity with the gaze of the male protagonist or hero" (Wright, *Feminism and Psychoanalysis: A Critical Dictionary*, 447–48).

western logocentric ideology: see **logocentrism**.

FILMOGRAPHY

Alien. Dir. Ridley Scott. Twentieth Century Fox/Brandywine, 1979.

Alien: Resurrection. Dir. Pierre Jeunet. Twentieth Century Fox/Brandywine, 1997.

Aliens. Dir. James Cameron. Twentieth Century Fox/Brandywine, 1986.

Alien³. Dir. David Fincher. Twentieth Century Fox/Brandywine, 1992.

Basic Instinct. Dir. Paul Verhoeven. Guild/Carolco/Canal+, 1992.

Blade Runner. Dir. Ridley Scott. Warner/Ladd/Blade Runner Partnership, 1982.

Blond Ambition Tour. Madonna. Boy Toy/Music Tours, 1992.

The Blue Angel. Dir. Josef von Sternberg. UFA, 1930.

The Bodyguard. Dir. Mick Jackson. Warner/Tig Productions/Kasdan Pictures, 1992.

Bulworth. Dir. Warren Beatty. Twentieth Century Fox, 1998.

Cabaret. Dir. Bob Fosse. AA-ABC Pictures Corp., 1972.

A Clockwork Orange. Dir. Stanley Kubrick. Warner/Polaris, 1971.

Dances with Wolves. Dir. Kevin Costner. Guild/Tig Productions/Jim Wilson, Kevin Costner, 1990.

Dead Man Walking. Dir. Tim Robbins. Working Title Films/Havoc/Gramercy, 1995.

Do the Right Thing. Dir. Spike Lee. UIP/Forty Acres and a Mule Filmworks/Spike Lee, 1989.

Dressed to Kill. Dir. Brian de Palma. Filmways/Samuel Z. Arkoff/Cinema 77, 1980.

Fires in the Mirror: Crown Heights, Brooklyn and Other Identities. Dir. George C. Wolfe. Written and performed by Anna Deavere Smith. PBS Video, 1993.

Mississippi Burning. Dir. Alan Parker. Rank/Orion, 1988.

Paris Is Burning. Dir. Jennie Livingston. ICA/Offwhite, 1990.

Rap City Rhapsody. Buchanan, Akili, producer. Current Affairs Dept., KQED, 1990.

Sammy and Rosie Get Laid. Dir. Stephen Frears. CineCom/Film Four, 1987.

The Silence of the Lambs. Dir. Jonathan Demme. Rank/Orion/Strong Heart/Demme, 1991.

Thelma and Louise. Dir. Ridley Scott. UIP/Pathé Entertainment, 1991.

Tongues Untied. Dir. Marlon Riggs. Graduate School of Journalism, UCB. KQED, Inc. First aired 11 June 1994.

Truth or Dare. Dir. Alex Kreshishian. Rank/Propaganda/Boy Toy, 1991.

Twilight—Los Angeles 1992. Written and performed by Anna Deavere Smith. First performed in 1992.

2001: A Space Odyssey. Dir. Stanley Kubrick. MGM/Stanley Kubrick, 1968.

Wag the Dog. Dir. Barry Levinson. Tribeca Productions/New Line Cinema, 1997.

Waiting to Exhale. Dir. Forest Whitaker. Twentieth Century Fox, 1995.

DISCOGRAPHY

Anderson, Laurie, and Roma Baran, producers. *Strange Angels*. With Laurie Anderson. Warner Brothers Records, 1989.

Davis, Clive, and Whitney Houston, executive producers. *The Bodyguard*. Original Soundtrack Album. Warner Brothers Records, 1992.

Edmonds, Kenneth "Babyface," Whitney Houston, and Clive Davis, executive producers. *Waiting to Exhale*. Original Soundtrack Album. Twentieth Century Fox, 1995.

Ice-T. "Copkiller" on *Body Count*. Time Warner, 1992.

Robbins, Tim, and David Robbins, executive producers. *Dead Man Walking*. Music from and Inspired by the Motion Picture. Sony Entertainment, 1995.

Sistah Souljah. *360 Degrees of Power*. Epic, 1992.

Skywalker, Luke, and 2 Live Crew. *As Nasty as They Wanna Be*. Skywalker Records, 1989.

BIBLIOGRAPHY

Abelove, Henry, Michèle Aina Barale, and David M. Halperin, eds. *The Lesbian and Gay Studies Reader*. New York: Routledge, 1993.

Abraham, Nicolas, and Maria Torok. *The Shell and the Kernel: Renewals of Psychoanalysis*. Chicago: University of Chicago Press, 1994.

———. *The Wolfman's Magic Word: Cryptonymy*. Minneapolis: University of Minnesota Press, 1986.

Althusser, Louis. *Lenin and Philosophy, and Other Essays*. Trans. Ben Brewster. New York: Monthly Review Press, 1972 [1971].

Amselle, Jean-Loup. *Logiques métisses: Anthropologie de l'identité en Afrique et ailleurs*. Paris: Payot, 1990.

Anderson, Benedict. *Imagined Communities: Reflections on the Origin and Spread of Nationalism*. New York: Verso, 1991.

Anzaldúa, Gloria. *Borderlands/La Frontera: The New Mestiza*, San Francisco: Spinsters/Aunt Lute, 1987.

Atwood, Margaret. *The Handmaid's Tale*. New York: Ballantine Books, 1987 [1985].

Baker, Houston, Manthia Diawara, and Ruth Lindeborg, eds. *Black British Cultural Studies: A Reader*. Chicago: University of Chicago Press, 1996.

Baldick, Chris. *The Concise Oxford Dictionary of Literary Terms*. Oxford: Oxford University Press, 1991.

Barker, Francis. *The Tremulous Private Body: Essays on Subjection*. New York: Methuen, 1984.

Basu, Rekha. "Sexual Imperialism: The Case of Indian Women in Britain." *Heresies* 12 (1981): 71–73.

Baudrillard, Jean. "The Ecstasy of Communication." Trans. John Johnson. In *The Anti-Aesthetic*, ed. Hal Foster, 126–34. Port Townsend, WA: Bay Press, 1983.

———. *Simulations*. Trans. P. Foss, P. Patton, and P. Beitchman. New York: Semiotext(e), 1983.

Bell, Laurie, ed. *Good Girls/Bad Girls: Sex Trade Workers and Feminists Face to Face*. Toronto: OPIRG, 1987.

Belsey, Catherine. *Critical Practice*. New York: Routledge, 1980.

Benedikt, Michael. Introduction to *Cyberspace: First Steps,* ed. M. Benedikt, 1–25. Boston: MIT Press, 1991.

Bersani, Leo. *The Culture of Redemption.* Cambridge: Harvard University Press, 1990.

———. "Is the Rectum a Grave?" In *AIDS: Cultural Analysis/Cultural Activism,* ed. Douglas Crimp, 197–222. Cambridge: MIT Press, 1988.

Bhabha, Homi K. "Signs Taken for Wonders." In *The Post-Colonial Studies Reader,* ed. Bill Ashcroft et al., 29–35. New York: Routledge, 1995.

———. "Postcolonial Authority and Postmodern Guilt." In *Cultural Studies,* ed. Lawrence Grossberg, Cary Nelson, and Paula Treichler, 56–68. New York: Routledge, 1992.

Bloom, Allan. *The Closing of the American Mind.* New York: Simon and Schuster, 1987.

Bly, Robert. *Iron John: A Book about Men.* Reading, MA: Addison-Wesley, 1990.

Bordwell, David, and Kristin Thompson. *Film Art: An Introduction.* New York: McGraw-Hill, 1993.

Brown, Wendy. "Toward a Genealogy of Moralism." In *Incorporations: Rhetoric, Critical Practice, and Public Culture,* ed. M. Deem. Forthcoming. Also in *Culturing Democracy,* ed. T. Keenan and K. Thomas. New York: Verso, forthcoming.

———. *States of Injury: Power and Freedom in Late Modernity.* Princeton: Princeton University Press, 1995.

Bruno, Giuliana. "Ramble City: Postmodernism and *Blade Runner.*" *October* 41 (summer 1987): 61–74.

Bukatman, Scott. *Terminal Identity: The Virtual Subject in Post-Modern Science Fiction.* Durham: Duke University Press, 1993.

Butler, Judith. *Excitable Speech: A Politics of the Performative.* New York: Routledge, 1997.

———. "Burning Acts: Injurious Speech." In *Deconstruction is/in America,* ed. Anselm Haverkamp, 149–80. New York: New York University Press, 1995.

———. "Against Proper Objects." *Differences: A Journal of Feminist Cultural Studies* 6, nos. 2–3 (summer-fall 1994): 1–26.

———. *Bodies That Matter: On the Discursive Limits of "Sex."* New York: Routledge, 1993.

———. "Critically Queer." *GLQ: A Journal of Lesbian and Gay Studies* 1, no. 1 (1993): 17–32.

———. *Gender Trouble: Feminism and the Subversion of Identity.* New York: Routledge, 1990.

Butler, Octavia E. *Xenogenesis Trilogy: Imago*. New York: Warner Books, 1989.

———. *Xenogenesis Trilogy: Adulthood Rites*. New York: Warner Books, 1988.

———. *Xenogenesis Trilogy: Dawn*. New York: Warner Books, 1987.

Califia, Pat, ed. *The Lesbian S/M Safety Manual*. Boston: Alyson Publications, 1988.

Carr, C. "Reclaiming Our Basic Rights." *Village Voice*, 28 April 1992, 35–36.

Case, Sue-Ellen. "Tracking the Vampire." *Differences: A Journal of Feminist Cultural Studies* 3, no. 2 (summer 1991): 1–20.

Certeau, Michel de. *Heterologies: Discourse on the Other*. Trans. Brian Massumi. Minneapolis: University of Minnesota Press, 1986.

Chabram-Dernersesian, Angie. "I Throw Punches for My Race, but I Don't Want to Be a Man: Writing US—Chica-nos (Girls, us)/Chicanas—into the Movement Script." In *Cultural Studies,* ed. Lawrence Grossberg, Cary Nelson, and Paula Treichler, 81–95. New York: Routledge, 1992.

Cherniavsky, Eva. "Subaltern Studies in a U.S. Frame." *boundary* 2 23, no. 2 (1996): 85–110.

Cisneros, Sandra. *Woman Hollering Creek*. New York: Vintage Books, 1991.

Cleaver, Eldridge. *Soul on Ice*. New York: McGraw-Hill, 1968.

Clifford, James. "Traveling Cultures." In *Cultural Studies,* ed. Lawrence Grossberg, Cary Nelson, and Paula Treichler, 92–116. New York: Routledge, 1992.

Clover, Carol. *Men, Women, and Chain Saws: Gender in the Modern Horror Film*. Princeton: Princeton University Press, 1992.

Conrad, Joseph. *Nostromo*. New York: Modern Library, 1983 [1951].

Crenshaw, Kimberlè Williams. "Beyond Racism and Misogyny: Black Feminism and 2 Live Crew." In *Words That Wound*, ed. Mari Matsuda et al., 111–32. Boulder: Westview, 1993.

Crimp, Douglas. "Portraits of People with AIDS." In *Cultural Studies,* ed. Lawrence Grossberg, Cary Nelson, and Paula Treichler, 117–33. New York: Routledge, 1992.

———. "How to Have Promiscuity in an Epidemic." *October* 43 (winter 1987): 237–70.

———, ed. *AIDS: Cultural Analysis/Cultural Activism*. Cambridge: MIT Press, 1988.

Culler, Jonathan. *On Deconstruction: Theory and Criticism after Structuralism*. Ithaca: Cornell University Press, 1982.

Dargis, Manohla. "*Alien³* and Its Metaphors." *Village Voice*, 30 June 1992, 64.

Davis, Angela. "Outcast Mothers and Surrogates: Racism and Reproductive

Politics in the Nineties." In *American Feminist Thought at Century's End,* ed. Linda S. Kauffman, 355–66. Cambridge, MA: Blackwell, 1993.

Dean, Tim. "The Psychoanalysis of AIDS." *October* 63 (winter 1993): 83–116.

Debord, Guy. *The Society of the Spectacle.* Detroit: Black and Red Press, 1983.

Delacoste, Frédérique, and Priscilla Alexander, eds. *Sex Work: Writings by Women in the Sex Industry.* Pittsburgh: Cleis Press, 1987.

De Lauretis, Teresa. *The Practice of Love: Lesbian Sexuality and Perverse Desire.* Bloomington: Indiana University Press, 1994.

Deleuze, Gilles, and Félix Guattari. *Anti-Oedipus: Capitalism and Schizophrenia.* Trans. R. Hurley, M. Seem, and H. Lane. Minneapolis: University of Minnesota Press, 1983.

Dent, Gina, ed. *Black Popular Culture.* A project by Michele Wallace. Seattle: Bay Press, 1992.

Derrida, Jacques. *Positions.* Trans. Alan Bass. Chicago: University of Chicago Press, 1981.

Diamond, Irene, and Lee Quinby, eds. *Feminism and Foucault: Reflections on Resistance.* Boston: Northeastern University Press, 1988.

Doherty, Thomas. "*Basic Instinct*: Politically Incorrect, Socially Irresponsible, Great Entertainment." *Cinefantastique* 23, nos. 2–3 (October 1992): 4–5.

Douglas, Mary. *Purity and Danger: An Analysis of Concepts of Pollution and Taboo.* New York: Praeger, 1988 [1966].

Dworkin, Andrea. *Intercourse.* New York: Free Press, 1987.

Ellis, Bret Easton. *American Psycho.* New York: Vintage Books, 1991.

———. "The Twentysomethings: Adrift in a Pop Landscape." *New York Times,* 2 December 1990, H1.

Elmer-DeWitt, Philip. "Cyberpunk!" *Time,* 8 February 1993, 58–65.

Fanon, Frantz. *The Wretched of the Earth.* Paris: Présence Africaine, 1963.

Feher, Michel, ed. with Ramona Naddaff and Nadia Tazi. *Fragments for a History of the Human Body.* Cambridge: MIT Press, 1989.

Feinberg, Leslie. *Stone Butch Blues: A Novel.* Ithaca, NY: Firebrand Books, 1993.

Fhaner, Beth A., and Christopher P. Scanlon, eds. *Magill's Cinema Annual, 1996.* 15th ed. Detroit: Gale, 1996.

Fiske, John. "Cultural Studies and the Culture of Everyday Life." In *Cultural Studies,* ed. Lawrence Grossberg, Cary Nelson, and Paula Treichler, 154–73. New York: Routledge, 1992.

———. "British Cultural Studies." In *Channels of Discourse: Television and Contemporary Criticism,* ed. Robert C. Allen, 254–89. Chapel Hill: North Carolina University Press, 1987.

————. *Television Culture.* New York: Methuen, 1987.

Fitting, Peter. "The Lessons of Cyberpunk." In *Technoculture,* ed. Constance Penley and Andrew Ross, 295–315. Minneapolis: University of Minnesota Press, 1991.

Foster, Hal, ed. *Discussions in Contemporary Culture: Number One.* Seattle: Bay Press, 1987.

————. *The Anti-Aesthetic: Essays on Postmodern Culture.* Port Townsend, WA: Bay Press, 1983.

Foucault, Michel. *The History of Sexuality.* Vol. 1, *An Introduction.* New York: Pantheon, 1986 [1978].

————. "The Discourse on Language." In *The Archaeology of Knowledge and the Discourse on Language.* Trans. A. M. Sheridan Smith, 215–37. New York: Harper Colophon Books, 1972.

Fradenburg, Louise, and Carla Freccero, eds. *Premodern Sexualities.* New York: Routledge, 1996.

Freccero, Carla. "Historical Violence, Censorship, and the Serial Killer: The Case of *American Psycho.*" *diacritics* 27, no. 2 (summer 1997): 44–58. Special Issue on Censorship, ed. Georges Van Den Abbeele.

————. "Bodies and Pleasures: Early Modern Interrogations." *Romantic Review* 86, no. 2 (March 1995): 379–90.

————. "Unruly Bodies: Popular Culture Challenges to the Regime of Body Backlash." *Visual Anthropology Review,* fall 1993, 74–81.

————. "Our Lady of MTV: Madonna's 'Like a Prayer.'" *Boundary 2* 19, no. 2 (summer 1992): 163–83. Special Issue on *Feminism and Postmodernism,* ed. Margaret Ferguson and Jennifer Wicke.

————. *Father Figures: Genealogy and Narrative Structure in Rabelais.* Ithaca: Cornell University Press, 1991.

————. "June Jordan." In *African American Writers,* ed. Valerie Smith, 245–61. New York: Charles Scribner's Sons, 1991.

————. "Notes of a Post–Sex Wars Theorizer." In *Conflicts in Feminism,* ed. Marianne Hirsch and Evelyn Fox Keller, 305–25. New York: Routledge, 1990.

Freud, Sigmund. "Fetishism (1927)." In *Sexuality and the Psychology of Love,* ed. Philip Rieff, 214–19. New York: Collier Books, 1970 [1963].

————. "The Uncanny (1919)." In *On Creativity and the Unconscious: Papers on the Psychology of Art, Literature, Love, Religion,* ed. Benjamin Nelson, 122–61. New York: Harper and Row, 1958.

————. "Mourning and Melancholia (1917)." In *General Psychological Theory: Papers on Metapsychology,* ed. Philip Rieff, 164–79. New York: Collier Books, 1963.

Frith, Simon. "The Cultural Study of Popular Music." In *Cultural Studies*, ed. Lawrence Grossberg, Cary Nelson, and Paula Treichler, 174–86. New York: Routledge, 1992.

Frith, Simon, and Angela McRobbie. "Rock and Sexuality." *Screen Education* 29 (1978–79): 3–19.

Gaitet, Pascale. *Political Stylistics: Popular Language as Literary Artifact*. New York: Routledge, 1992.

Garber, Marjorie B. *Vested Interests: Cross-Dressing and Cultural Anxiety*. New York: Routledge, 1992.

Gates, Henry Louis, Jr. *Loose Canons: Notes on the Culture Wars*. New York: Oxford University Press, 1992.

———. "2 Live Crew, Decoded." *New York Times*, 19 June 1990, A23.

Gerard, Jeremy. "David Hwang: Riding on the Hyphen." *New York Times Magazine*, 13 March 1988, 44.

Gibson, William. *Neuromancer*. New York: Ace Books, 1984.

Giddens, Anthony. "The Globalising of Modernity." In *Colonial Discourse and Post-Colonial Theory: A Reader,* ed. Patrick Williams and Laura Chrisman, 181–89. New York: Columbia University Press, 1994.

———. *The Consequences of Modernity*. Cambridge, MA: Polity Press, 1990.

Gilroy, Paul. *The Black Atlantic: Modernity and Double Consciousness*. Cambridge: Harvard University Press, 1993.

———. *"There Ain't No Black in the Union Jack"*: *The Cultural Politics of Race and Nation*. Chicago: University of Chicago Press, 1991 [1987].

Gire, Dan. *"Silence of the Lambs*: Anthony Hopkins on Hannibal Lecter." *Cinéfantastique* 23, nos. 2–3 (October 1992): 108–9.

Glover, David, and Cora Kaplan. "Guns in the House of Culture: Crime Fiction and the Politics of the Popular." In *Cultural Studies,* ed. Lawrence Grossberg, Cary Nelson, and Paula Treichler, 213–26. New York: Routledge, 1992.

Godzich, Wlad. "Foreword: The Further Possibility of Knowledge." In Michel de Certeau, *Heterologies: Discourse on the Other,* trans. Brian Massumi, vii–xxi. Minneapolis: University of Minnesota Press, 1986.

Goldberg, Jonathan, ed. *Reclaiming Sodom*. New York: Routledge, 1994.

Gomez, Jewelle. *The Gilda Stories: A Novel*. Ithaca, NY: Firebrand Books, 1991.

Grossberg, Lawrence, Cary Nelson, and Paula Treichler, eds. *Cultural Studies*. New York: Routledge, 1992.

Grosz, Elizabeth. *Volatile Bodies: Towards a Corporeal Feminism*. Bloomington: Indiana University Press, 1994.

Grover, Jan Zita. "AIDS, Keywords, and Cultural Work." In *Cultural Studies,* ed. Lawrence Grossberg, Cary Nelson, and Paula Treichler, 227–39. New York: Routledge, 1992.

Halberstam, Judith. "Skinflick: Posthuman Gender in Jonathan Demme's *The Silence of the Lambs.*" *Camera Obscura* 27 (September 1991): 37–52.

Hall, Stuart. "Cultural Studies and Its Theoretical Legacies." In *Cultural Studies,* ed. Lawrence Grossberg, Cary Nelson, and Paula Treichler, 277–94. New York: Routledge, 1992.

———. "Encoding and Decoding." In *Culture, Media, Language,* ed. Stuart Hall et al., 128–38. London: Hutchinson, 1980.

Hall, Stuart, and Paddy Whannel. *The Popular Arts.* Boston: Beacon Press, 1967 [1964].

Halliwell, Leslie. *Halliwell's Film Guide.* 10th ed. Ed. John Walker. New York: Harper Perennial, 1995.

Haraway, Donna. "The Promises of Monsters: A Regenerative Politics for Inappropriate/d Others." In *Cultural Studies,* ed. Lawrence Grossberg, Cary Nelson, and Paula Treichler, 295–337. New York: Routledge, 1992.

———. "The Biopolitics of Postmodern Bodies." In *Simians, Cyborgs, and Women,* 203–30. New York: Routledge, 1991.

———. "A Cyborg Manifesto: Science, Technology, and Socialist-Feminism in the Late Twentieth Century." In *Simians, Cyborgs, and Women,* 149–81. New York: Routledge, 1991.

———. *Simians, Cyborgs, and Women: The Reinvention of Nature.* New York: Routledge, 1991.

———. "Situated Knowledges: The Science Question in Feminism and the Privilege of Partial Perspective." In *Simians, Cyborgs, and Women,* 183–201. New York: Routledge, 1991.

Harlow, Barbara. *Resistance Literature.* New York: Methuen, 1987.

Harris, Daniel. "Make My Rainy Day." *Nation,* 8 June 1992, 790–93.

Harris, Thomas. *The Silence of the Lambs.* New York: St. Martin's, 1988.

Haverkamp, Anselm, ed. *Deconstruction is/in America: A New Sense of the Political.* New York: New York University Press, 1995.

Hebdige, Dick. *Subculture: The Meaning of Style.* New York: Routledge, 1991.

Hernandez, Gilbert. *Flies on the Ceiling/Los Bros Hernandez.* Vol. 9. Seattle: Fantagraphics Books, 1991.

———. *Heartbreak Soup and Other Stories.* Westlake Village, CA: Fantagraphics Books, 1987.

Hernandez, Jaime. *Love and Rockets: Short Stories/Los Bros Hernandez.* Westlake Village, CA: Fantagraphics Books, 1987.

Hirsch, E. D. *Cultural Literacy: What Every American Needs to Know.* Boston: Houghton Mifflin, 1987.

Hirsch, Marianne, and Evelyn Fox Keller, eds. *Conflicts in Feminism*. New York: Routledge, 1990.

Hitchens, Christopher. "Minority Report." *Nation*, 7 January 1991, 7.

Hoare, Quintin, and Geoffrey Nowell Smith, eds. and trans. *Selections from the Prison Notebooks of Antonio Gramsci*. New York: International Publishers, 1972.

Holden, Stephen. "Madonna Re-Creates Herself—Again." *New York Times*, 19 March 1989.

Holmlund, Christine. "*Down and Out in Beverly Hills, Rocky IV, Aliens*: New Cold War Sequels and Remakes." *Jump Cut* 35 (n.d.): 85–96.

Honderich, Ted, ed. *The Oxford Companion to Philosophy*. Oxford: Oxford University Press, 1995.

hooks, bell. *Black Looks: Race and Representation*. Boston: South End Press, 1992.

———. "Is Paris Burning?" In *Black Looks: Race and Representation*, 145–56. Boston: South End Press, 1992.

———. "Madonna: Plantation Mistress or Soul Sister?" In *Black Looks: Race and Representation*, 157–64. Boston: South End Press, 1992.

———. "Representing Whiteness in the Black Imagination." In *Cultural Studies*, ed. Lawrence Grossberg, Cary Nelson, and Paula Treichler, 338–46. New York: Routledge, 1992.

———. "Counter-Hegemonic Art: *Do the Right Thing*." In *Yearning: Race, Gender and Cultural Politics*, 173–84. Boston: South End Press, 1990.

———. *Yearning: Race, Gender and Cultural Politics*. Boston: South End Press, 1990.

———. "Feminism: A Transformational Politic." In *Talking Back/Thinking Black*, 19–27. Boston: South End Press, 1989.

Iannone, Carol. "PC and the Ellis Affair." *Commentary* 91, no. 1 (July 1991): 52.

Jackson, Earl, Jr. "Desire at Cross(-Cultural) Purposes: *Hiroshima, Mon Amour* and *Merry Christmas, Mr. Lawrence*." *Positions* 2, no. 1 (spring 1994): 133–74.

Jameson, Fredric. *Postmodernism, or, The Cultural Logic of Late Capitalism*. Durham: Duke University Press, 1991.

———. "Postmodernism, or The Cultural Logic of Late Capitalism." *New Left Review* 146 (July-August 1984): 53–92.

———. "Postmodernism and Consumer Society." In *The Anti-Aesthetic*, ed. Hal Foster, 111–25. Port Townsend, WA: Bay Press, 1983.

———. "Magical Narratives: On the Dialectical Use of Genre Criticism." In *The Political Unconscious*, 103–50. Ithaca: Cornell University Press, 1981.

————. *The Political Unconscious: Narrative as a Socially Symbolic Act.* Ithaca: Cornell University Press, 1981.

————. *The Prison-House of Language: A Critical Account of Structuralism and Russian Formalism.* Princeton: Princeton University Press, 1972.

Jordan, June. "Waiting for a Taxi." In *Technical Difficulties: African American Notes on the State of the Union,* 161–68. New York: Vintage Books, 1994.

————. *Moving towards Home: Political Essays.* London: Virago, 1989.

————. *Civil Wars.* Boston: Beacon Press, 1981.

Kalin, Tom. "Slant: Tom Kalin on Queer Nation." *Artforum* 29, no. 3 (November 1990): 21–23.

Kaplan, Cora. *Sea Changes: Culture and Feminism.* London: Verso, 1986.

Kauffman, Linda S., ed. *American Feminist Thought at Century's End: A Reader.* Cambridge, MA: Blackwell, 1993.

Kavanaugh, James. "'Son of a Bitch': Feminism, Humanism, and Science in *Alien.*" *October* 13 (summer 1980): 91–100.

Keller, Evelyn Fox. *Reflections on Gender and Science.* New Haven: Yale University Press, 1985.

Kipnis, Laura. "(Male) Desire and (Female) Disgust: Reading *Hustler.*" In *Cultural Studies,* ed. Lawrence Grossberg, Cary Nelson, and Paula Treichler, 373–91. New York: Routledge, 1992.

Kroker, Arthur, and Marilouise Kroker, eds. *The Hysterical Male: New Feminist Theory.* Basingstoke: Macmillan Education, 1991.

Lacan, Jacques. "The Signification of the Phallus." In *Ecrits: A Selection,* trans. Alan Sheridan, 281–91. Paris: Editions du Seuil, 1966.

Laplanche, Jean. *Problématiques II: Castration–Symbolisations.* Paris: Presses Universitaires de France, 1980.

Laplanche, Jean, and J.-B. Pontalis. *The Language of Psychoanalysis.* Trans. Donald Nicholson-Smith. New York: Norton, 1973 [1967].

Lee, Spike, with Lisa Jones. *Do the Right Thing: A Spike Lee Joint.* New York: Fireside, 1989.

Lentricchia, Frank, and Thomas McLaughlin, eds. *Critical Terms for Literary Study.* Chicago: University of Chicago Press, 1990.

Lewis, Lisa A. *Gender Politics and MTV: Voicing the Difference.* Philadelphia: Temple University Press, 1990.

Lionnet, Françoise. *Postcolonial Representations: Women, Literature, Identity.* Ithaca: Cornell University Press, 1995.

Longino, Helen E., and Evelyn Hammonds. "Conflicts and Tensions in the Feminist Study of Gender and Science." In *Conflicts in Feminism,* ed. Marianne Hirsch and Evelyn Fox Keller, 164–83. New York: Routledge, 1990.

Lorde, Audre. *From a Land Where Other People Live*. Detroit: Broadside Press, 1973.

Love, Robert. "Psycho Analysis." *Rolling Stone*, 4 April 1991, 45.

Lyotard, Jean-François. *The Postmodern Condition: A Report on Knowledge*. Trans. Geoff Bennington and Brian Massumi. Minneapolis: University of Minnesota Press, 1984.

Madonna. *Sex*. New York: Warner Books, 1992.

Mailer, Norman. "The Children of the Pied Piper." *Vanity Fair*, March 1991, 154.

Malcomsin, Scott L. "Socialism or Death?" *New York Times Magazine*, 25 September 1994, 44.

Marder, Elissa. "*Blade Runner*'s Moving Still." *Camera Obscura* 27 (September 1991): 89–107.

Marin, Louis. *Utopiques: Jeux d'espaces*. Paris: Editions de Minuit, 1973.

Martin, Biddy. "Sexualities without Genders and Other Queer Utopias." *Diacritics* 24, nos. 2–3 (summer-fall 1994): 104–21.

Marx, Karl. *Capital*. Vol. 1. Trans. Ben Fowkes. New York: Vintage, 1977.

Matsuda, Mari, Charles Lawrence, Richard Delgado, and Kimberlè Crenshaw, eds. *Words That Wound: Critical Race Theory, Assaultive Speech, and the First Amendment*. Boulder: Westview, 1993.

McClintock, Anne. "The Angel of Progress: Pitfalls of the Term 'Post-colonialism.'" In *Colonial Discourse and Post-Colonial Theory: A Reader,* ed. Patrick Williams and Laura Chrisman, 291–304. New York: Columbia University Press, 1994.

———. "Screwing the System: Sexwork, Race, and the Law." *Boundary 2* 19, no. 2 (summer 1992): 70–95. Special Issue on *Feminism and Postmodernism,* ed. Margaret Ferguson and Jennifer Wicke.

McMillan, Terry. *Waiting to Exhale*. New York: Viking, 1992.

McRobbie, Angela. *Feminism and Youth Culture: From Jackie to Just Seventeen*. Boston: Unwin Hyman, 1991.

Mercer, Kobena. *Welcome to the Jungle: New Positions in Black Cultural Studies*. New York: Routledge, 1994.

———. "'1968': Periodizing Postmodern Politics and Identity." In *Cultural Studies,* ed. Lawrence Grossberg, Cary Nelson, and Paula Treichler, 424–49. New York: Routledge, 1992.

Mies, Maria. *Patriarchy and Accumulation on a World Scale: Women in the International Division of Labour*. London: Zed Books, 1986.

Minh-ha, Trinh. *See* Trinh.

Mitchell, Juliet, and Jaqueline Rose, eds. Introduction to *Feminine Sexuality:*

Jacques Lacan and the Ecole Freudienne, trans. Jaqueline Rose. London: Macmillan, 1982.

Mohanty, Chandra. "Under Western Eyes: Feminist Scholarship and Colonial Discourses." In *Colonial Discourse and Post-Colonial Theory: A Reader,* ed. Patrick Williams and Laura Chrisman, 196–220. New York: Columbia University Press, 1994.

———. "Introduction: Cartographies of Struggle, Third World Women and the Politics of Feminism." In *Third World Women and the Politics of Feminism,* ed. Chandra Mohanty, Anne Russo, and Lourdes Torres, 1–47. Bloomington: University of Indiana Press, 1991.

Mohanty, Chandra, Anne Russo, and Lourdes Torres, eds. *Third World Women and the Politics of Feminism.* Bloomington: University of Indiana Press, 1991.

Moore, Lorrie. "Trashing Women, Trashing Books." *New York Times,* 5 December 1990.

Moraga, Cherríe. *Loving in the War Years.* Boston: South End Press, 1983.

Morris, William, ed. *The American Heritage Dictionary of the English Language.* New York: American Heritage, 1969.

Mulvey, Laura. *Visual and Other Pleasures.* Bloomington: University of Indiana Press, 1989.

Murphy, Kathleen. "The Last Temptation of Sigourney Weaver." *Film Comment* 28, no. 4 (July–August 1992): 17–20.

Nava, Michael. *How Town: A Novel of Suspense.* New York: Harper and Row, 1990.

The New Lexicon: Webster's Dictionary of the English Language. New York: Lexicon Publications, 1989.

Orsi, Robert A. *The Madonna of 115th Street: Faith and Community in Italian Harlem.* New Haven: Yale University Press, 1985.

Palacios, Monica. "La Llorona Loca: The Other Side." In *Chicana Lesbians: The Girls Our Mothers Warned Us About,* ed. Carla Trujillo, 49–51. Berkeley: Third Woman Press, 1991.

Parker, Andrew, Mary Russo, Doris Sommer, and Patricia Yeager, eds. *Nationalisms and Sexualities.* New York: Routledge, 1992.

Patton, Cindy. *Sex and Germs: The Politics of AIDS.* Boston: South End Press, 1985.

Penley, Constance. "Feminism, Psychoanalysis, and the Study of Popular Culture." In *Cultural Studies,* ed. Lawrence Grossberg, Cary Nelson, and Paula Treichler, 479–500. New York: Routledge, 1992.

Penley, Constance, and Andrew Ross. "Cyborgs at Large: Interview with

Donna Haraway." In *Technoculture,* ed. Constance Penley and Andrew Ross, 1–19. Minneapolis: University of Minnesota Press, 1991.

Persons, Dan. "*Silence of the Lambs*: Jonathan Demme on Filming the Shocker That Made Movie Horror Respectable." *Cinefantastique* 23, nos. 2–3 (October 1992): 107–11.

Radway, Janice. "Reading Is Not Eating: Mass-Produced Literature and the Theoretical, Methodological, and Political Consequences of a Metaphor." *Book Research Quarterly* 2, no. 3 (fall 1986): 9–29.

Rall, Ted. "Meet the Cusp Kids." *New York Times,* 25 April 1995.

Reagon, Bernice. "Coalition Politics: Turning the Century." In *Home Girls: A Black Feminist Anthology,* ed. Barbara Smith, 356–69. New York: Kitchen Table/Women of Color Press, 1983.

Ricoeur, Paul. *Freud and Philosophy.* Trans. Denis Savage. New Haven: Yale University Press, 1970.

Roiphe, Rebecca, and Daniel Cooper. "Batman and the Jewish Question." *New York Times,* 2 July 1992, A17.

Rosaldo, Renato. *Culture and Truth: The Remaking of Social Analysis.* Boston: Beacon Press, 1989.

Rosenblatt, Roger. "Snuff This Book! Will Bret Easton Ellis Get Away with Murder?" *New York Times Book Review,* 16 December 1990, 3.

Ross, Andrew. "New Age Technoculture." In *Cultural Studies,* ed. Lawrence Grossberg, Cary Nelson, and Paula Treichler, 531–47. New York: Routledge, 1992.

———. "Hacking Away at the Counterculture." In *Technoculture,* ed. Constance Penley and Andrew Ross, 107–34. Minneapolis: University of Minnesota Press, 1991.

———. *No Respect: Intellectuals and Popular Culture.* New York: Routledge, 1989.

Rubin, Gayle. "Thinking Sex: Notes for a Radical Theory of the Politics of Sexuality." In *The Lesbian and Gay Studies Reader,* ed. Henry Abelove, Michèle Aina Barale, and David M. Halperin, 3–44. New York: Routledge, 1993. First published in Carole S. Vance, ed., *Pleasure and Danger.* Boston: Routledge and Kegan Paul, 1984.

———. "The Traffic in Women: Notes toward a Political Economy of Sex." In *Toward an Anthropology of Women,* ed. Rayna Reiter, 157–210. New York: Monthly Review Press, 1975.

Rushkoff, Douglas, ed. *The GenX Reader.* New York: Ballantine Books, 1994.

Saakana, Amon Saba. "Mythology and History: An Afrocentric Perspective of the World." *Third Text* 3–4 (1988): 143–50.

Said, Edward. *Culture and Imperialism.* New York: Knopf, 1993.

———. *Orientalism*. New York: Vintage Books, 1979.

SAMOIS, ed. *Coming to Power: Writings and Graphics on Lesbian S/M.* Boston: Alyson Publications, 1982.

Santoro, Gene. "How 2 B Nasty." *Nation*, 2 July 1990, 4–5.

Schiebinger, Londa. *The Mind Has No Sex? Women in the Origins of Modern Science*. Cambridge: Harvard University Press, 1989.

Schulman, Sarah. *People in Trouble*. New York: Dutton Books, 1990.

———. "AIDS and Homelessness." *Nation*, 10 April 1989, 480–82.

Scobie, Stephen. "What's the Story, Mother? The Mourning of the Alien." *Science-Fiction Studies* 20, no. 1 (March 1993): 80–93.

Sedgwick, Eve Kosofsky. "Queer Performativity: Henry James's *The Art of the Novel.*" *GLQ: A Journal of Lesbian and Gay Studies* 1, no. 1 (1993): 1–16.

———. *Between Men: English Literature and Male Homosocial Desire*. New York: Columbia University Press, 1985.

Shell, Marc. *The Economy of Literature*. Baltimore: Johns Hopkins University Press, 1978.

Shewey, D. "The Gospel according to Madonna." *Advocate*, 21 May 1991, 40.

Simonson, Rick, and Scott Walker, eds. *The Graywolf Annual Five: Multi-Cultural Literacy: Opening the American Mind*. Saint Paul, MN: Graywolf Press, 1988.

Sofia, Zoë. "Exterminating Fetuses: Abortion, Disarmament, and the Sexo-Semiotics of Extraterrestrialism." *Diacritics* 14, no. 2 (summer 1984): 47–59.

Spillers, Hortense. "Mama's Baby, Papa's Maybe: An American Grammar Book." *Diacritics* 17, no. 2 (1987): 65–81.

———. "Interstices: A Small Drama of Words." In *Pleasure and Danger*, ed. Carole S. Vance, 73–100. Boston: Routledge and Kegan Paul, 1984.

Spivak, Gayatri Chakravorti. "Imperialism and Sexual Difference." In *Contemporary Literary Criticism: Literary and Cultural Studies,* ed. Robert Con Davis and Ronald Schleifer, 517–29. New York: Longman, 1989.

Spivak, Gayatri Chakravorti, with Ellen Rooney. "In a Word. Interview." *Differences: A Journal of Feminist Cultural Studies* 1, no. 2 (summer 1989): 124–56.

Stevens, Robin. "Love and Rockets." *Out/Look*, spring 1992, 32–33.

Stone, Allucquere Rosanne. "Will the Real Body Please Stand Up? Boundary Stories about Virtual Cultures." In *Cyberspace: First Steps,* ed. Michael Benedikt, 81–118. Boston: MIT Press, 1991.

Strick, Philip. "*Alien³.*" *Sight and Sound* 2, no. 4 (August 1992): 40.

Taubin, Amy. "Invading Bodies: *Alien³* and the Trilogy." *Sight and Sound* 2, no. 3 (July 1992): 8–10.

Taubin, Amy. "The Boys Who Cried Misogyny." *Village Voice*, 28 April 1992, 35–36.

———. "Killing Men (Serial Killers in Motion Pictures)." *Sight and Sound* 1, no. 1 (May 1991): 14–18.

Tomlinson, John. *Cultural Imperialism*. Baltimore: Johns Hopkins University Press, 1991.

Trinh T. Minh-ha. *Woman, Native, Other: Writing Postcoloniality and Feminism*. Bloomington: University of Indiana Press, 1989.

———. "Not You/Like You: Post-Colonial Women and the Interlocking Questions of Identity and Difference." *Inscriptions* 3–4 (1988): 71–77.

Turner, Graeme. *British Cultural Studies: An Introduction*. 2d ed. New York: Routledge, 1996.

———. *British Cultural Studies: An Introduction*. Boston: Unwin Hyman, 1990.

Turner, Kay. *I Dream of Madonna: Women's Dreams of the Goddess of Pop*. San Francisco: Collins Publishers, 1993.

Vance, Carol S., ed. *Pleasure and Danger: Exploring Female Sexuality*. Boston: Routledge and Kegan Paul, 1984.

Van Meter, Jonathan. "Madonna's Boyz Express Themselves to Jonathan Van Meter." (Interview) *New York Quarterly* 1 (26 January 1992): 13.

Verdier, Raymond. "Chercher remède à l'excision: Une nécessaire concertation." *Droit et cultures* 20 (1990): 149.

Vickers, Nancy. "Maternalism and the Material Girl." In *Embodied Voices: Representing Female Vocality in Western Culture*, ed. Leslie C. Dunn and Nancy A. Jones. Cambridge: Cambridge University Press, 1994.

———. "Vital Signs: Petrarch and Popular Culture." *Romanic Review* 79, no. 1 (1988): 184–95.

Virilio, Paul. "Aliens." In *Zone: Incorporations,* ed. Jonathan Crary and Sanford Kwinter, 446–49. New York: Unzone, 1992.

Walker, Alice. *The Color Purple*. New York: Washington Square Press/Pocket Books, 1982.

Wallace, Michele. "Negative Images: Towards a Black Feminist Cultural Criticism." In *Cultural Studies,* ed. Lawrence Grossberg, Cary Nelson, and Paula Treichler, 654–71. New York: Routledge, 1992.

———. *Invisibility Blues*. New York: Verso, 1990.

———. *Black Macho and the Myth of the Superwoman*. New York: Dial Press, 1979.

Wallerstein, Immanuel. *The Modern World-System I: Capitalist Agriculture and the Origins of the European World-Economy in the Sixteenth Century*. New York: Academic Press, 1974.

Warner, William. "Spectacular Action: Rambo and the Popular Pleasures of Pain." In *Cultural Studies,* ed. Lawrence Grossberg, Cary Nelson, and Paula Treichler, 672–88. New York: Routledge, 1992.

Weber, Bruce. "Sigourney Weaver in Alien Terrain . . . Yet Again." *New York Times,* 17 May 1992, H15.

Weeks, Jeffrey. *Sexuality and Its Discontents: Meanings, Myths, and Modern Sexualities.* Boston: Routledge, 1989 [1985].

Will, George. "Slamming the Doors." *Newsweek,* 25 March 1991, 65–66.

Williams, Patrick, and Laura Chrisman, eds. *Colonial Discourse and Post-Colonial Theory: A Reader.* New York: Columbia University Press, 1994.

Williams, Raymond. *Keywords: A Vocabulary of Culture and Society.* New York: Oxford University Press, 1985 [1976].

Wood, Robert E. "Cross Talk: The Implications of Generic Hybridization in the *Alien* Films." *Studies in the Humanities* 15 (1988): 1–12.

Wood, Robin. "Return of the Repressed." *Film Comment* 14, no. 4 (1978): 25–32.

Wright, Elizabeth, ed. *Feminism and Psychoanalysis: A Critical Dictionary.* Oxford: Blackwell, 1992.

Young, Elizabeth. "*The Silence of the Lambs* and the Flaying of Feminist Theory." *Camera Obscura* 27 (September 1991): 5–35.

Žižek, Slavoj. *Enjoy Your Symptom! Jacques Lacan in Hollywood and Out.* New York: Routledge, 1992.

———. *Looking Awry: An Introduction to Jacques Lacan through Popular Culture.* Cambridge: MIT Press, 1991.

———. "Eastern Europe's Republics of Gilead." *New Left Review* 183 (1990): 50–62.

———. *The Sublime Object of Ideology.* London: Verso, 1989.

INDEX

accountability, of cultural producer, 81–82
activism, and cultural studies, 22, 137*n*. 19
aesthetics: and loss of oppositional force,
90; postmodern, 100
African American *(see also* Black *entries)*;
vs. Black, 136*n*. 6
African, as symbol, 90, 110
AIDS: and *Alien³*, 123–125, 128–129,
147*n*. 29; in *Aliens,* 123; and valorization of death drive, 128–129
alien(s): in *Alien,* 114; in *Alien³*, 127–
128; in *Alien* films, 111; in *Aliens,*
119–120, 122, 146*n*. 18
Alien³ (Kavanaugh and Weaver), 123–129,
147*n*. 28, 148*n*. 35; AIDS and gay discourse in, 123–125, 128–129, 147*n*. 29;
nationalism in, 125–126, 129; self-sacrifice and death in, 125–129, 147*n*. 33
Alien (Scott), 111–115, 146*n*. 18; gender
in, 114–115; spectatorship of, 123;
technology in, 113–114, 116–117
Alien films, 111, 146*n*. 14
Alien: Resurrection, 136*n*. 9, 146*n*. 14
Aliens (Cameron), 115–123, 146–147*n*.
22; gender in, 118–121; nationalism in,
118–119, 122–123; race in, 121–122,
146*n*. 18; spectatorship of, 123; technology in, 116–118
Althusser, Louis: definition of ideology,
137*n*. 10; interpellation concept of, 18
analysis, of popular culture: close reading
in, 22–23; critical, 17–18, 22–23; as cultural studies project, 4, 17, 20; film,
23–24; identifying contradictions in, 8;
literary techniques of, 6; locating oneself
as analyst, 17–18; and political action,
22–23, 137*n*. 19; reasons for, 2–5, 12;
as resistance to social control, 20
analyst, of popular culture: as critic,
17–18; self-awareness of, 17–18, 22–23
Anderson, Laurie, 112

art: mass vs. popular, 135*n*. 1, 135–136*n*.
8; "obscene," debates on funding for,
33–34
artist *(see* cultural producer)
As Nasty as They Wanna Be (2 Live
Crew), 89
Atwood, Margaret, 33–34

Basic Instinct (Verhoeven), 8, 23–25; gender and sexuality in, 24–26
Bildungsroman, 68
binary oppositions, 70–71; inversion of,
61; valorization of first term in, 71,
141*n*. 16
bisexuality, in *Basic Instinct,* 24
Black (term), 136*n*. 6
Black men: cultural production by, 82; in
Madonna's productions, 56; and sexism, 82
Black political struggles: and *Do the Right
Thing,* 86–87; masculinity in, 78–79;
and other identity struggles, 60
Black women: in Madonna productions,
53–54; representations of and by, 51; in
Waiting to Exhale, 94–95
Blackness: commodification of, 16–17,
62–63; as symbol of natural and authentic, 53, 90, 110
Blacks: in *Alien³*, 125–126; "heroic" self-
sacrifice of, 125–126; and Madonna,
52–56; and military, 121–122; and rap,
88–89; and whiteness, 74
Blade Runner (Scott), 100–102
Bloom, Allan, 3
body(ies): in cyberspace, 104–105, 110;
disenfranchised, 35; Madonna's representations of, 46–47; multiple social
meanings of, 60; in *Neuromancer,*
109–110; social control of, 19–20; and
state, 33–35, 39–40; women's, state
control of, 33–34, 39

Carla Freccero, who was trained in early modern history and literature, is a professor in the departments of literature, women's studies, and the history of consciousness at the University of California, Santa Cruz. She received her B.A. from Harvard in 1977 and her Ph.D. from Yale in 1984, specializing in Renaissance studies. Freccero's books include *Father Figures: Genealogy and Narrative Structure in Rabelais*; and *Premodern Sexualities*, coedited with Louise Fradenburg. She has published numerous essays on Renaissance texts and on cultural politics and U.S. popular culture, including an entry on June Jordan for *African American Writers*; "Notes of a Post–Sex Wars Theorizer"; "Unruly Bodies: Popular Culture Challenges to the Regime of Body Backlash"; "Our Lady of MTV: Madonna's 'Like a Prayer'"; and "Historical Violence, Censorship, and the Serial Killer: The Case of *American Psycho*."